THE NATIONAL GALLERY

# THE NATIONAL GALLERY

*A Short History*

Charles Saumarez Smith

**F**

FRANCES LINCOLN LIMITED
PUBLISHERS

*For Ferdinand*

THE NATIONAL GALLERY
Frances Lincoln Limited
4 Torriano Mews
Torriano Avenue
London NW5 2RZ
www.franceslincoln.com

ISBN: 978-0-7112-3043-9

Printed and bound in China
by South China Printing Co. Ltd

2 4 6 8 9 7 5 3 1

**1005826140**

# CONTENTS

*Introduction*                                    7

1   *Origins*                                    12

2   *William Seguier*                            31
    *1824–43*

3   *Charles Eastlake*                           55
    *1843–7*

4   *Thomas Uwins*                               61
    *1847–55*

5   *Sir Charles Eastlake*                       67
    *1855–65*

6   *Sir William Boxall*                         81
    *1865–74*

7   *Sir Frederic Burton*                        86
    *1874–94*

8   *Sir Edward Poynter*                         95
    *1894–1904*

9   *Sir Charles Holroyd*                       101
    *1906–16*

10  *Sir Charles Holmes*                        113
    *1916–28*

11   *Sir Augustus Daniel*                    *119*
     *1928–32*

12   *Sir Kenneth Clark*                      *123*
     *1934–45*

13   *Sir Philip Hendy*                       *133*
     *1945–68*

14   *Sir Martin Davies*                      *143*
     *1968–74*

15   *Sir Michael Levey*                      *146*
     *1974–86*

16   *Neil MacGregor*                         *153*
     *1987–2002*

*Envoi*                                       *164*

*Bibliography*                                *173*

*Acknowledgements*                            *181*

*Index*                                       *183*

# INTRODUCTION

I remember the day that I became Director of the National Gallery, walking through the black, staff door to the left of the main entrance portico, down the corridor and past the ranks of display boards which record the names of former Trustees painted in letters of gold, past the portrait by Sir Thomas Lawrence of John Julius Angerstein, whose collection formed the original National Gallery, to the Director's Office, once occupied by Sir Kenneth Clark, who filled it with works of art from his private collection and kept his salary cheques uncashed in the drawers of his desk.

It was immediately obvious that the National Gallery is an institution which has a strong sense of its own history, steeped in a view of its primacy at the heartland of British culture and, in particular, of the roll-call of its Trustees, beginning with the Earl of Liverpool as Prime Minister. But this history has in the past been curiously under-articulated, as if the institution does not wish particularly to analyse or investigate the circumstances of its formation in order to present itself as in some way eternal. A sense and feeling for the past is formidably present in the underlying culture of the institution, in its deep conservatism and self-belief, as well as determining the shape and character of its collection according to the tenets of the western European canon. But these beliefs are not much discussed: they are ever-present in forming the collection, but assumed not to be open to questioning.

I discovered that there was no very easy way of finding out how the National Gallery had come into being, how it had developed, and, in particular, what were the character and personality of my predecessors as Directors, whose existence is nowhere inscribed in the institution, and many of whom are unexpectedly forgotten. There was then no easily accessible book about the National Gallery, other than a small introduction, hard to obtain, which was co-written by Charles Holmes, the only other Director before me to have previously been Director of the National Portrait Gallery, and by Charles Collins Baker, Keeper of the National Gallery during the 1920s, which was published to celebrate the National Gallery's centenary in 1924.

I quickly discovered that I was far from being alone in lamenting the absence of an official history. In May 1999, Nicholas Penny, then Keeper, now my successor as Director, had established a seminar to encourage research into the history of museums and of the National Gallery in particular. Chris Whitehead, a lecturer at the University of Newcastle-on-Tyne, had recently completed a Ph.D. thesis on the debates and disputes surrounding the mid-Victorian National Gallery, which has since been published as *The Public Art Museum in Nineteenth Century Britain: The Development of the National Gallery*. Jonathan Conlin had been appointed to a research fellowship at Sidney Sussex College, Cambridge to convert his Ph.D. thesis on the early history of the National Gallery into a full-length book. David Cannadine, the brilliant historian of late nineteenth- and twentieth-century historical culture, had been encouraged by my predecessor, Neil MacGregor, to consider writing an official history, but had sadly turned the suggestion down. Nicholas Penny was himself writing the biographical entries on early collectors (a number of whom were Trustees or Directors), which were subsequently published as appendices to his two catalogues of *Sixteenth-Century Italian Paintings*. And Alexander Sturgis had been asked by the National Gallery's trading company to write a short illustrated history to give visitors a sense of the institution and of its past.

When Sturgis left to become the Director of the Holburne Museum in Bath, I rashly volunteered to take over the task. I thought it would provide an opportunity to find out more about a set of issues and questions in which I had become interested: how the National Gallery had come into being; how the circumstances of its foundation had shaped its subsequent history; who my predecessors as Directors were and what their personality had been; how and when the pictures had been acquired and, perhaps more especially, how they had been paid for; what was the relationship between the National Gallery and the government of the time; and, finally, since I was trained as an architectural historian, what was the history of the building in which the collection had been displayed.

Not long after I began work, Jonathan Conlin published his very substantial and admirably well researched and documented history under the title *The Nation's Mantelpiece: A History of the National Gallery*. It provides a full analytical and scholarly history of the National Gallery and of the politics of its operation. But I decided to persevere with this shorter and much more personal narrative of the history of the National Gallery in the hope that it would provide answers to some of those questions which I had asked when I arrived as Director in 2002.

I have based my narrative on the periods of office of the Directors who preceded me. Historians of museums, including Conlin, will regard this as an old-fashioned approach, since it presumes that the Directors are the people who shape the character of the institution, more than the impersonal politics of staffing, finance, audiences and ideology. Sadly, I have not really been able to provide a set of detailed character studies. I would love to know more about what my predecessors thought and felt as they sat in the office in the south-west corner of the building or walked through the galleries after hours, but their mind-set is frequently unexpectedly opaque and hard to identify behind the impersonal façade of official memoranda. But, I hope that the sequence of Directors at the very least provides a convenient armature to the narrative and a record of their contribution to the life of the institution.

It has always struck me that Directors of institutions (not just the National Gallery) influence how an institution operates far beyond what they actually do and say and that staff are inclined to mould their actions to what they perceive as the priorities of the person in charge. As Director, I certainly was conscious of treading in the footsteps of my predecessors, facing many of the same challenges, and aware that they had themselves grappled with many of the same issues of government under-funding, what the National Gallery can reasonably be expected to buy, how to extend the shape of the collection, and of sometimes tricky staff and Trustee relations. In particular, it will be obvious to anyone reading the history that I became increasingly interested as I wrote the book in the vexed issue of the relationship between the Directors and their Boards of Trustees and how, throughout so much of the history of the National Gallery, this has proved unexpectedly tense, Trustees so often feeling that they have a duty to second-guess the ideas of their Directors, to decide and criticise acquisitions, to ignore changes in public taste, and to treat their Directors with ill-concealed contempt.

In fact, I realise in retrospect, now that the history has been written and now that I have myself left the post of Director of the National Gallery to be Secretary and Chief Executive of the Royal Academy of Arts, that one reason for writing this history was as a way of consoling myself that the problems I faced were no different from those of my predecessors:

that the culture of the institution and its *modus operandi*, the character of the collection and the relationship to its audience, are all to a considerable extent shaped and determined by its history. The National Gallery is not static and unchanging. It has been subject to changing ideas and beliefs and social attitudes. It is itself a construction of history.

# I. ORIGINS

The National Gallery should really have been founded during the 1760s as part of the enlightenment desire to provide public instruction through institutions of fine art. This was the period when George III first began to take an interest in how to encourage the arts through the foundation of the Royal Academy of Arts, and when John Wilkes, a radical and habitually argumentative MP, was agitating amongst the members of the Society of Artists for 'a great Museum all our own'.

But the British parliament has always had a slightly wary attitude towards the arts, generally feeling – except for a period in the mid-nineteenth century – that they should depend on private initiative, rather than public enterprise, and, at least in the eighteenth century, it certainly did not want to extend public expenditure beyond the traditional preoccupations of the state with fighting wars abroad and the safety of the realm. As a result of this timidity on the part of both the crown and parliament, the origins of the National Gallery in Great Britain are very different from those of museums and galleries on the continent, the majority of which were founded during the second half of the eighteenth century as an act of largesse on the part of monarchs and minor princes, enabling the public to see works of art previously held by royal collections.

In continental Europe, the Hapsburgs opened the Belvedere Gallery down at the bottom of their formal garden in the then suburbs of Vienna and Augustus the Strong built the Zwinger in Dresden. Meanwhile, a public gallery was opened in Düsseldorf in 1710 by the Palatine Elector and a picture gallery was attached to Frederick the Great's great palace at Sanssouci in Potsdam near Berlin. In Kassel, the Museum Fridericianum opened in 1769. By contrast, Great Britain had to wait until the early 1820s for its National Gallery, after the foundation of the Louvre in Paris and the Prado in Madrid, after the German principalities had converted their princely collections into public institutions, after the Swedish royal family had opened the doors and catalogued the collections of its Royal Palace, after the citizens of Antwerp had assembled the paintings which came from parish churches in the city into a museum, and some time after individuals had paved the way for the creation of public collections in Great Britain, including the opening of Dulwich picture gallery in 1813 and the foundation of the Fitzwilliam Museum in 1816.

While there was no National Gallery before 1824, there had been a long period of public discussion as to why there should be one, at least since the sale in 1779 of Sir Robert Walpole's collection of paintings from his country house at Houghton, which provoked the first occasion of public outrage that great works of art were being exported abroad and not kept for the enjoyment of the British public.

There was a feeling then, as there has been ever since, that if a great collection of works of art in this country is sold, particularly if it has some particular association with this country – Walpole had, after all, been Prime Minister – then it should be kept in Britain for public enjoyment and, more especially, for the education of artists. This idea of the education of public taste has remained at the heart of arguments about a National Gallery.

Once the germ of the idea had been planted, it recurred with increasing regularity in the rhetoric surrounding state promotion of the arts in the late eighteenth century. The madcap Irish artist James Barry, one of only two artists ever to have been expelled from the Royal Academy, is known to have promoted the idea of a 'National Gallery' when he became Professor of Painting at the Royal Academy in 1782. He appealed to the belief, which became a common theme, that it was much easier to study Old Master paintings on the continent and particularly in France. In 1794 the Louvre was made into a public institution for the enjoyment of its collections, which spurred the British to take an interest in the idea, since it was felt that whatever the French did, the English could do at least as well, if not better. In particular, the sale in London in 1798 of the astonishing collection of French and Italian paintings which had previously belonged to the Duc d'Orléans led to a movement to persuade parliament to buy the collection in its entirety and present it to the Royal Academy, so that it could be available for artists to study. Benjamin West, the President of the Royal Academy and close ally of George III, put the case to the King that it should consist of

> a noble collection for young artists to refer to without being obliged to go to Paris after a peace to study such works as the French have collected, and where with their studies they would suck in political principles ill calculated for England.

But the government then, as so often since, decided that it could not afford the Orléans collection, a great lost opportunity which the current government has cause to lament owing to the extraordinary cost of the paintings now which were once part of it. Instead, it was sold to a private consortium, consisting of some of the great moguls of the late eighteenth-century aristocracy – the Duke of Bridgewater, fortified by his great wealth from canals and coal-mines, his nephew the Earl Gower (later second Marquess of Stafford and Duke of Sutherland) and Gower's brother-in-law, the Earl of Carlisle, who owned great estates in Cumberland and round Newcastle as well as Castle Howard. An exhibition of some of the works, including the works by Titian and Poussin now in the Sutherland collection on loan to the Scottish National Gallery, was held in the Lyceum Hall in the Strand and in Pall Mall.

From this point onward, there was endless, highly vocal lobbying for a National Gallery. Joseph Farington, the artist and diarist, argued that the Orléans collection should become a study facility for artists, and Charles Long, Joint Secretary to the Treasury and an ally of the Prime Minister, William Pitt, talked to him about the idea, which was only rejected on grounds of 'necessities of state'.

In 1790 Prince Michael Poniatowski, the brother of the King of Poland, came to London and persuaded a French merchant and art collector, Noel Desenfans, to help him to put together a collection of paintings which could form the basis of a National Gallery in Warsaw. Desenfans was astute and had good connections in France, so was able to assemble an important group of works of art. In 1799, he wrote 'A Plan for Establishing a National Gallery', in which he suggested, unsuccessfully, that the British government might add his paintings to the British Museum.

There was much discussion about Desenfans's proposal, some of it recorded in Joseph Farington's diary. He provides a long entry for 17 January 1799 in which he describes how:

> The subject of Desenfans pamphlet was talked of. –
> Malone said He had talked to a Trustee of the Museum
> who said that some years ago something of the same
> kind was proposed, which caused the Archbishop
> of Canterbury to call a meeting of the Trustees who

decided against it. – Desenfans said that was on acct.
of a proposal of the Duke of Richmond to sell his
collection of Statues to the Nation to be placed in
the British Museum. Northcote said the Trustees of
the Museum were sure to oppose any scheme which
proposed to alter their establishment. – I gave as my
opinion that such a measure as that of Mr. Desenfans
could only be carried by *Sap*, that is by possessing the
minds of Mr. Long, Mr. Rose and such persons as
are abt. and familiar with Mr. Pitt, and who in their
domestic intercourse satisfy him of the advantages
which wd. result from such a scheme. – That I wd. give
up every idea of interfering with the establishment of
the British Museum, as the opposition of the Trustees
wd. in a great measure be avoided, – and the purpose be
equally well attained, by only annexing to the Museum
such buildings as might be necessary, so as to connect
as a *National Depot* a Museum of Arts as well as of
Literature and Curiosities.

Farington subsequently recorded how the idea had been discussed with the Archbishop of Canterbury and, in February
1799, how John Hoppner had suggested to Charles Long that
the paintings should go, instead, to the Royal Academy.

In 1805, instead of a National Gallery being established
by act of parliament, a group of private individuals, mostly
wealthy collectors, decided to found the British Institution. It
was intended to combine the functions of showing the work
of contemporary British artists with occasional displays of
Old Master paintings and occupied the premises on Pall Mall
which had previously been used for John Boydell's Shakespeare
Gallery and was essentially a monument to private enterprise.
It was probably not an accident that it opened in the year of
the Battle of Trafalgar, since it was self-consciously patriotic

in its aspirations, sponsoring competitions to commemorate Britain's naval victories and describing its purpose as being 'to form a PUBLIC GALLERY of the works of British Artists, with a few select specimens of each of the great schools'.

As with the sale of the Orléans Collection, the opening of the British Institution prompted further calls for government support for the arts and, in 1806, the playwright Richard Brinsley Sheridan petitioned parliament for £5,000 a year 'for the encouragement of art', believing that 'a country like this ought to show the world that in war as well as in peace, we should carry on everything for the greatness and benefit of the Country'.

The next step on the long road to the founding of the National Gallery came about with the death of Noel Desenfans in 1807. He left his collection of works of art to a long-standing friend and *protégé*, Sir Francis Bourgeois (he had been knighted in Poland), who was determined that they should be made available to the public. He was reported to want to offer the collection 'to the Nation, upon condition that Parliament should vote that a Building sh[ould] be erected to receive them, & of size sufficient to admit another Collection of equal number'. It was assumed that he would leave the collection to the British Museum, but he apparently disliked the way the British Museum was run. In 1810 he tried to buy the freehold of a house in Charlotte Street in order that the house 'may be gratuitously open to artists as well as to the publick' and, in his will drawn up in 1810, he bequeathed the collection instead to Noel Desenfans's widow with the stipulation that it should be left in due course to Dulwich College. Bourgeois died on 8 January 1811. As a result of his will, the first public art gallery in Britain opened in Dulwich in a building designed by Sir John Soane and including a mausoleum containing the remains of Noel Desenfans and Sir Francis Bourgeois.

One of the key figures in lobbying government to give greater support to the arts was Sir George Beaumont, a Leicestershire landowner, member of the so-called Committee of Taste chaired by Charles Long to commission monuments for the nation and, in 1805, one of the founders of the British Institution. In 1812 he confided in Farington that, if a National Gallery were to be formed, he would be prepared to leave to it his collection of paintings. In the same year, he dedicated an urn to the memory of Reynolds in the grounds of Coleorton Hall. Influenced by the teaching of Reynolds, Beaumont believed passionately that the study of the Old Masters was essential to the healthy development of a school of modern British painting.

Another key figure was John Julius Angerstein, the illegitimate son of a British merchant in St Petersburg and a prominent figure in marine insurance (he was one of the founders of Lloyd's), who, like Beaumont, was a major collector. Like Beaumont, he bought contemporary British paintings as well as Old Masters, acquiring Hogarth's aggressively individualistic and self-consciously patriotic self-portrait, *The Painter and his Pug*, in 1792 and Hogarth's great series of modern morality stories about the decline and fall of a wastrel, young aristocrat, *Marriage A-la-Mode*, in 1795. At the sale of the Orléans Collection in 1798, he bought Sebastiano del Piombo's enormous and deeply religious painting of *The Raising of Lazarus*, one of the largest works of art ever to have left Italy, having been exported from Rome to Narbonne cathedral in the sixteenth century. It hung upstairs in the great room of his house on Pall Mall. In June 1809, he acquired Rembrandt's *The Woman taken in Adultery* for 4,000 guineas (an enormous sum) on the recommendation of Sir Thomas Lawrence.

Both Beaumont and Angerstein had been able to benefit from the opening up of the international market for Old

Master paintings as a result of the Napoleonic Wars, the looting of collections in Italy by Napoleon's army, the sale and capture of works of art in Spain, and by the displacement of works of art from churches following the French Revolution. The much freer circulation of works of art in the first decade of the nineteenth century led to a corresponding interest in the study and examination of paintings by artists, dealers and collectors and the creation of a much more active art market in London. Whereas in the eighteenth century, an interest in Old Master painting tended to be confined to those members of the nobility who had been on the Grand Tour and who might, for example, have been members of the Society of Dilettanti, in the first two decades of the nineteenth century, there was a much broader interest in art, more artists, and the beginnings of a literature of art criticism, as demonstrated by the writings of William Hazlitt.

However, at the time, this growing public interest in seeing and studying Old Master paintings was satisfied only by the occasional exhibition at the British Institution or by visiting the galleries of private houses, for example in Thomas Hope's Duchess Street Mansion or the gallery belonging to the Marquess of Stafford (formerly Lord Gower), designed by Charles Heathcote Tatham and attached to Cleveland House off Green Park. Lord Stafford's Gallery was available to be seen by anyone known to the Marquess on Wednesday afternoons in May, June and July and a catalogue was published in 1808 by John Britton.

So, what happened to change the mind of the government and persuade them that it might be a good idea to establish a National Gallery?

In 1821, George Beaumont visited Italy, where he had been in the early 1780s with his wife on the Grand Tour. The visit convinced him of the great benefits of the public having free access to works of art. On 27 December 1821, he wrote to his friend, the poet William Wordsworth:

> the Vatican & the Capitol are opened quite gratuitously
> to every rank, & it is delightful to see people of all
> descriptions from the highest to the lowest gazing at
> works which in London would not be regarded with
> half the pleasure with which our people devour the
> Panorama or Mrs Salmons waxwork.

This passage, inspired by his visits to the Capitoline Museum in Rome and the Museo Pio-Clementino in the Vatican, encapsulates many of the ideas which lay behind the establishment of the National Gallery: the belief that Britain ought to be able to afford improving pleasures, which were readily available in cities on the continent, in contrast to the much more ephemeral pleasures of panoramas and waxworks.

Beaumont returned to London determined to use his considerable influence behind the scenes to establish a National Gallery. In November 1822, he approached Sir Charles Long, who had been involved in all the discussions about establishing a National Gallery, about the possibility of establishing a gallery of paintings as part of the British Museum, where Long was a Trustee. The following May 1823, Beaumont was made a Trustee of the British Museum and both he and Long were appointed to a sub-committee 'to consider a proper building for the Reception of the Royal Library and a Picture Gallery over it', to be part of the British Museum's new building designed by Robert Smirke. In the same month, George Agar Ellis, a young, handsome Whig MP, came to visit Beaumont at his house in Grosvenor Square and Beaumont persuaded him to talk to the Prime Minister about the idea of a public gallery to house Beaumont's collection.

Meanwhile, John Julius Angerstein died in January 1823. The circle of connoisseurs and collectors who had been keen to establish a National Gallery feared that his collection would be sold abroad and it was rumoured to be on offer to the Prince of Orange for £70,000.

Events now began to move quite fast. On 1 July 1823, Agar Ellis announced in the House of Commons that he was going to propose that the government should buy Angerstein's collection. The suggestion was greeted by cheers. He noted in his diary:

> Went to the House of Commons, where I found Croker
> making a foolish and at the same time illnatured
> attack on the Trustees of the British Museum – I spoke
> shortly in their defence – praised Sir George Beaumont
> for his generous intention . . . & gave notice of my
> intention early next session to propose to Parliament
> to vote a sum of money to buy Angerstein's collection
> for the public – Ridley Colborne – Alexander Baring
> – & Wortley supported me – & the House cheered, &
> seemed on the whole favourably disposed towards my
> proposition.

When the sub-committee of the British Museum trustees met on 11 July to discuss Smirke's plans for the new museum building, they agreed that space should be set aside on the first floor of the east wing to provide 'a temporary arrangement of any collection of paintings that may be formed in the Museum . . . till the proposed gallery in the opposite wing . . . is built . . .' In other words, the Trustees of the British Museum must have recognised that there was a strong public mood for the Museum to accommodate paintings and, now that public money was in the offing for the purchase of the Angerstein Collection, decided that they should provide space. On the following day, at a meeting of the full Board of Trustees, Charles Long submitted a list of the paintings that Beaumont was planning to give. On 17 July, Beaumont clarified his intentions in a letter to the Board, in which he revealed that he would give sixteen paintings to the nation 'whenever the Gallery about to be erected is ready to receive them'.

By September 1823, Lord Liverpool, the Prime Minister, was himself persuaded that a National Gallery should be established. On 19 September, he wrote to Angerstein's son, John, stating that the nation wished to acquire the collection belonging to his father in order to establish a National Gallery. On the same day, he told the Duchess of Devonshire that 'We are about to lay the foundation of a National Gallery, by the purchase of Mr Angerstein's Pictures – You know that Sir Geo Beaumont has announced his intention of leaving his Pictures to the Public & I am persuaded that when a Gallery is established there will be many bequests'.

By December 1823, the executors of Angerstein's will had agreed to sell thirty-eight of the paintings from his collection to the government for £57,000, a valuation which was provided by William Seguier, a well known figure in the art world and Superintendent of the British Institution, who worked as a dealer and adviser to collectors, including the Duke of Wellington and Viscount Fitzwilliam.

On 27 January 1824, George Beaumont wrote to George Agar Ellis:

> By easy access to such works of art the public taste must improve, which I think the grand desideratum: for, when the time shall come when bad pictures . . . shall be neglected, and excellence never passed over, my opinion is we shall have fewer painters and better pictures.

This passage is an indication of the issues which were being considered in connection with the opening of the National Gallery: the improvement of public taste was paramount; and the study of Old Master painting was expected to improve the taste of the current generation of painters, such that – as Beaumont put it – 'we shall have fewer painters and better pictures'.

The improvement of public taste and the opportunities a National Gallery would provide for the training of artists are the *leitmotifs* through all the public discussion during 1823 and 1824. Beaumont wanted artists to paint like the hero of his youth, Sir Joshua Reynolds, who was fascinated by Old Master paintings, and not like Turner, who was regarded by Beaumont as too radical and subversive, too immune to the influence of the past. This was one of the key issues which divided people about the possible benefits of a National Gallery. Some thought that it would improve the practice of art. Others were more sceptical. Constable, who wanted to paint from nature, believed that a National Gallery would corrupt contemporary art and wrote to his friend John Fisher, the archdeacon of Salisbury that

> Should there be a National Gallery there will be an
> end of the art in poor old England . . . the reason is
> plain; the manufacturers of pictures are then made the
> criterions of perfection, instead of nature.

On 23 February 1824, the Chancellor of the Exchequer, Frederick Robinson (nicknamed 'Prosperity' Robinson), stood up in parliament to make his budget speech. He announced

> the establishment of a splendid gallery of works of art,
> worthy of the nation; – a gallery, on the ornaments of
> which, every Englishman who paces it may gaze with

the proud satisfaction of reflecting, that they are not the rifled treasures of plundered palaces, or the unhallowed spoils of violated altars.

England's National Gallery was not to be the Louvre, which was regarded as being, to too great an extent, the result of Napoleon's victories in Italy. He also alluded to a

> Valuable collection at present in the possession of a high-spirited individual . . . which through his liberality, would be likely to find its way to a National Gallery. Should this prove to be the case, I am sanguine in my hope that the noble example would be followed by many similar acts . . . the result of which will be the establishment of a splendid Gallery . . . worthy of the Nation.

One catches in the rhetoric of this budget speech some of the sense of urgency behind the establishment of the National Gallery: the belief that it would be a monument to Britain's position in the world. More prosaically, the financing of the National Gallery was made possible by the return of a loan of £70,000 which had been made to the Austrian government in 1816.

The next issue which had to be faced was whether or not the National Gallery should be free-standing or attached to the British Museum. During the previous summer, there had been a coalition of interests between John Cam Hobhouse, a Radical and friend of Byron, John Croker, a Tory essayist, and Sir James Mackintosh, a Whig, to prevent the British Museum housing the national collection of paintings. In March 1824, this group renewed their pleas as to the inappropriateness of the British Museum as a destination for paintings, given that, as Alexander Baring had argued, 'the mixture of antiquity, books, natural history, and Marbles in the Museum' was already 'a most jumbling and incongruous arrangement' and 'the works of art should be in a gallery by themselves'. Croker claimed that only a centrally located Gallery could 'civilize and humanize the public at large'.

On 23 March 1824, the purchase of Angerstein's collection was announced to the House of Commons and, on 30 March, a Treasury Minute reported the appointment of William Seguier as Keeper. A grant of £60,000 to cover the purchase of Angerstein's house and its contents in Pall Mall to house the National Gallery was voted on 2 April 1824. Agar Ellis posed the question:

> If there were any gentlemen in that House who
> disapproved of the expense that these pictures were
> putting the country, he would ask them, whether they
> might not be productive of emolument to the nation,
> even in a pecuniary point of view?

Agar Ellis expanded his views on the virtues and expectations of a National Gallery in an article published in April 1824 in the *Quarterly Review*. It is only now, at the moment that the National Gallery is about to open, that consideration is given to the benefits which might be afforded to a broader public beyond the circle of connoisseurs, collectors and artists, who up until this point had been regarded as its natural public. Agar Ellis was specific as to who would benefit from convenient public access to works of art:

> [This] acquisition . . . forms undoubtedly a most
> important era in the history of arts in this country
> . . . Our artists might, possibly, have gone and studied in
> Italy . . . [but] the great body of the people, the middling
> classes, as well as very many of the higher orders could

not . . . have done this; and therefore, their only chance of becoming acquainted with what is really fine art, was the establishment of a National Gallery.

He continued:

> To have a gallery of paintings generally and frequently seen, there must be no sending for tickets . . . its doors must be always open, without fee or reward, to every decently dressed person; it must not be placed in an unfrequented street, nor in a distant quarter of town. To be of use, it must be situated in the very gangway of London, where it is alike accessible and conveniently accessible to all ranks and degrees of men – to the merchant, as he goes to his counting house – to the peers and the commons, on their way to the respective houses of parliament and to the men of literature and science, on their way to the respective *societies*, to the King and the Court . . . to the frequenter of clubs of all denominations – to the hunters of exhibitions (a numerous class in the metropolis) – to the indolent as well as to the busy – to the idle as well as the industrious.

Here, towards the end of the discussion about the establishment of a National Gallery, is a much more democratic vision of its potential audience. The Gallery was expected to be situated in 'the gangway of London', in other words in the comparative helter-skelter of Pall Mall, rather than the more remote purlieus of Bloomsbury, which was then regarded as too far from the centre of town. The middle classes, as well as the frequenters of clubs, were to be stimulated, as well as refreshed, by regular access to works of art.

The Treasury ordered that the Gallery was to be open four days a week from ten o'clock to five o'clock, with two further days, Friday and Saturday, set aside for copyists. The Gallery is said to have opened to the public in Angerstein's house in Pall Mall for the first time on 10 May 1824, but Agar Ellis visited it on 5 May and commented on the fact that the public were able to enter 'freely without tickets, being the first attempt at a perfectly open exhibition in this country. Seguier [the Keeper], whom I met there, told me the experiment succeeded perfectly – and that all the people are very orderly and well-behaved'. Benjamin Robert Haydon remarked that 'It was delightful to walk into the Gallery just as you felt inclined without trouble or inconvenience' and declared the government's purchase and public display of the collection to be 'the greatest step since the Elgin Marbles'.

It is clear, then, that a mixture of motives lay behind the foundation of the National Gallery: a combination of patriotism and public interest with a perhaps mistaken belief on the part of George Beaumont that the study of the Old Masters would ensure that British painting would develop through the study of the past. In particular, there has always been a certain ambiguity about the nature of the intended audience: does the National Gallery exist essentially for the education of artists? Or for the enjoyment of connoisseurs and collectors who already have an established interest in Old Master painting? Or for the benefit of a broader, more democratic public, including the poor? In practice, it has existed for all three, but the chemistry between the three and the priority which should be attached to their different needs has not always been straightforward.

In describing the ideas and beliefs of George Beaumont, it is important to remember that he was born in the mid-eighteenth century, a property owner in Leicestershire. His motives in the establishment of the National Gallery were essentially those of a traditional connoisseur, who had been taught drawing at Eton by Alexander Cozens, was a friend of the circle of artists involved in the establishment of the British Institution, and who collected paintings by his friends, as well as Old Masters, for his London house. In reading about the way he and his friends operated, it is clear that they belonged to a close-knit art establishment with close links to the House of Commons and shared artistic tastes. He was interested in the development of a British school of painting and thought that the National Gallery was the best way to do this.

Charles Long's attitudes are less scrutable. As a ubiquitous public servant with a genuine taste for the arts and a finger in every public project in the early part of the nineteenth century, he probably believed that it was legitimate for the state to fund a National Gallery as an extension of its public and fiduciary responsibilities, as well as a way of marking Britain's military supremacy in Europe in the aftermath of the Battle of Waterloo. So, a second strand in the formation of the National Gallery was the beginning of a consciousness on the part of government that it had a responsibility towards the education and welfare of the private citizen, alongside a sense of national pride, which had been evident in the purchase of the Elgin Marbles and which continued to be manifest in the martial decoration of the National Gallery's façade and its place on Trafalgar Square. When the Earl of Liverpool, who was the Prime Minister at the time of the foundation of the National Gallery and a Tory, had his portrait painted by Sir Thomas Lawrence in 1827, he asked that the painting should show him holding the charter of foundation of the National Gallery. This is evidence of the sense of national, as well as personal, pride which lay behind the foundation of a so-called 'National Gallery'.

George Agar Ellis was slightly more visionary and belonged to a younger generation of Whigs who believed in the benefits of public education and had a more democratic idea as to how the National Gallery might operate and to whom it should be available.

This was the mixture of motives and ideas and beliefs that lay behind the National Gallery: some concerned with the education of artists; some with the pleasure the collection might give to the educated; and some with the benefits it might provide to a broader public.

Later historians of the National Gallery have tended to narrow down the motives of the National Gallery in ways which can sometimes seem dangerously unhistorical. Social historians are inclined to think that it was an attempt on the part of the elite to provide an essentially aristocratic pleasure to the lower classes, the actions of an entrenched social oligarchy in providing a fortress of traditional culture and, indeed, it cannot be disguised that there is a curious tension in the history of the National Gallery between it being treated as the prerogative and preserve of a very narrow and extremely wealthy social class and its broader and more democratic mandate. Some of the secondary commentary about the foundation of the National Gallery imputes motives which belong more naturally to the later nineteenth century – to the idea of public and moral improvement more obviously associated with the writings of John Ruskin and other mid-nineteenth-century writers about the relationship between religion and art.

But, in truth, George Beaumont's ideas were probably more self-interested. He merely wanted a permanent home for his collection, so that it could be seen and enjoyed by fellow artists and connoisseurs as an extension of the Grand Tour tastes of his era. The atmosphere of the early National Gallery was as much private as public, lodged in Angerstein's private house in Pall Mall close to the Athenaeum and Travellers' Club, which were established in the same decade. Reading about the circumstances of its origins does not make one feel that it was intended to be especially democratic, nor was the audience very different in kind or character from the members of the gentleman's clubs nearby.

Viewed retrospectively from the vantage point of the twenty-first century, the foundation of the National Gallery can be seen to belong to a particular political and social climate, which was strongly oligarchic. On the one hand, it was a remarkable and far-sighted piece of public enterprise on the part of a cash-strapped Tory government, which had the prescience to realise how regular access to works of art might contribute to public education. At the same time, it is quite obviously a product of early nineteenth-century attitudes as to what constituted the greatest works of art and how these might influence public taste.

## 2. WILLIAM SEGUIER
## 1824-43

The Trustees of the National Gallery appointed William Seguier as its first Keeper, an entirely predictable choice as he was already very closely associated with the circle of artists and patrons who had been involved in its foundation. Born in the parish of St Martin-in-the-Fields in 1772, Seguier, whose father had been a picture dealer, was apparently trained as an artist by George Morland, but gave up painting after marrying in 1797. From this point onwards, he was an energetic and ubiquitous busybody in the art world, part-dealer, part-restorer, part-connoisseur, and a member of a group of artists known as 'The Clique', which included George Beaumont, David Wilkie, the historical painter, and Benjamin Robert Haydon, whose diaries provide such a valuable record of the period.

His Trustees may have respected Seguier's views on art, but, reading about the way that they operated, he seems to have been treated as a factotum, expected to work to their instructions and much later remembered by Lord Monteagle as always displaying 'a certain degree of reserve of manner, from the different positions of the parties'. Indeed, from this point onwards, it is clear that the relationship between the Trustees and the staff, including the Directors, has tended to be that of masters to their servants, an attitude of mind which was inscribed into the original circumstances of foundation. Seguier's letter of appointment described his duties as follows:

> To have the charge of the Collection and to attend particularly to the preservation of the Pictures: –

To Superintend the arrangements for admission,
when the same shall have been determined upon: –
To be present occasionally in the Gallery, and to
value and negotiate (if called upon) the purchase of any
Picture that may in future be added to the Collection.

The real authority in managing the affairs of the Gallery lay
with a 'Committee of Six Gentlemen' who were given the task
to 'undertake the superintendence of the National Gallery of
pictures, and to give such directions as may be necessary from
time to time, to Mr. Seguier, who will be instructed to con-
form to their orders'. The Trustees were Robert Jenkinson,
second Earl of Liverpool, as Prime Minister; Frederick
Robinson, the Chancellor of the Exchequer; George Gordon,
fourth Earl of Aberdeen, a highly intelligent scholar, who
had studied the Renaissance while at university, gothic architecture while in France, and had tried to buy the Parthenon
frieze before the Earl of Elgin; Sir Charles Long, Earl of
Farnborough, the descendant of a family of merchants in the
West Indies and *eminence grise* in providing advice about
matters of taste to George IV; Sir George Beaumont; and Sir
Thomas Lawrence, the most prominent and successful portrait painter of the day and President of the Royal Academy,
who had himself offered his services as Keeper 'being desir-
ous to save the pictures from the spoliation of cleaning and
restoring'. The dynamics of their relationship were the subject of a letter to *The Times* on 23 March 1826, in which
Sir Charles Long was described as 'the chief director', aided
by Seguier, 'the picture-cleaner'. Lord Aberdeen, Sir George
Beaumont and Sir Thomas Lawrence were regarded as 'mere
ciphers', while Beaumont was said to talk too much.

Meanwhile, the essential character of the National Gallery's
collection of paintings was formed by the taste of the two
individuals whose collections had led to its foundation. John

Julius Angerstein had been a classic wealthy collector who had chosen to invest his considerable fortune in art alongside many and various acts of public charity. George Beaumont was a more traditional country landowner with an interest in Old Master paintings and a painter himself. Neither was particularly scholarly in his interests. They were not much concerned by documentation or provenance or the idea of an art-historical narrative, but, instead, were preoccupied by issues of quality and by the ways in which their collections could demonstrate their own personal judgment. Indeed, the collection of the National Gallery can in some ways still be seen to bear the imprint of a period when a love of art was inspired by the Grand Tour, by classical literature and mythology, by a literary view of landscape, and by a passion for travel abroad; and there has always been a certain amount of debate amongst the Trustees as to whether it is a collection pre-eminently of great works of art only (the view normally taken by the Board of Trustees) or whether it is expected to illustrate a broader and more evidently didactic art historical narrative (the view of the professional staff).

The portion of Angerstein's collection which had been acquired for the National Gallery consisted of thirty-seven works (if one counts each of Hogarth's *Marriage A-la-Mode* series as a single work), including no fewer than five great paintings by Claude Lorrain, whose works had always been regarded as central to Grand Tour taste and had informed the English style of landscape gardening. He owned the *Landscape with Cephalus and Procris* (NG 2) and *A Seaport* (NG 5), which he acquired together from the dealer Philippe Panné in March 1805 for £4,500 and which were so much admired by J.M.W. Turner as a young man that he required his pictures to be hung alongside them in his will; the *Landscape with the Marriage of Isaac and Rebecca* (NG 12) and the *Seaport with the Embarkation of the Queen of Sheba* (NG 14), also acquired as a pair in April 1803 for 8,000 guineas; and the *Seaport with the Embarkation of Saint Ursula* (NG 30), bought by William Lock, a fellow collector, from the Palazzo Barberini in the early 1750s and sold to Angerstein in 1802.

The key work in Angerstein's collection and the foundation stone of the National Gallery's collection was Sebastiano del Piombo's huge painting of *The Raising of Lazarus* (NG 1). He also owned Raphael's *Portrait of Pope Julius II* (NG 27), Rubens's *The Rape of the Sabine Women* (NG 38), Rembrandt's *The Woman taken in Adultery* (NG 45) and *The Adoration of the Shepherds* (NG 47), and three Van Dycks, including the *Portrait of George Gage with Two Attendants* (NG 49). When the Scottish picture dealer William Buchanan saw the collection in November 1802, he described it as 'the most select of any Collection in any single room in London'.

Beaumont's collection was equally strong in Claudes, including the *Landscape with Narcissus and Echo* (NG 19), which he had bought at Christie's in 1790 for 500 guineas, the *Landscape with a Goatherd and Goat* (NG 58) and the *Landscape with Hagar and the Angel* (NG 61), the first Claude to be seen and admired by Constable, when Beaumont took it with him on a visit to Dedham. Like Angerstein, Beaumont owned a Rembrandt, *The Lamentation over the Dead Christ* (NG 43), which he acquired for 40 guineas from Sir Joshua Reynolds, and an even greater Rubens, *An Autumn Landscape with a View of Het Steen in the Early Morning* (NG 66), which Beaumont's wife had given him as a present in June 1803 and which he regarded as 'the finest landscape I believe he ever painted'. He also owned *The Stonemason's Yard* (NG 127), a beautiful view of the backyards of Venice by Canaletto, painted early in his career as a demonstration of his skill as an artist.

Beaumont did not claim any great consistency in his collecting. He bought works by the artists he admired to display either in the picture gallery which he built in 1792 attached to his town house in Grosvenor Square or at Coleorton Hall, his gothicised country house in Leicestershire. He told William Gilpin, the writer on art, that that his collection 'ranged from flower to flower'. In other words, it did not aspire to be a collection founded on historical principles and he had no interest, as did some collectors like William Roscoe in Liverpool, in early Italian or German painting. Indeed, viewed in terms of the history of taste, the National Gallery can be viewed as an assertion of the primacy of the classical tradition from Raphael to Correggio just at the moment when other collectors, artists and critics were beginning to be interested in artists of the fifteenth century, the so-called 'primitives'.

Acquisitions in the early years of the Gallery tended to follow the character of the two founding collections – not surprisingly since the Trustees very much shared the same tastes as Beaumont and were part of the same circle of collectors and connoisseurs. The first acquisition was Correggio's *Madonna of the Basket* (NG 23), a very lively, small painting in exceptionally good condition of the Christ-child with a slip of a shirt pulled up over the top of his body. It had been bought on 19 April 1825, just under a year after the National Gallery had opened its doors to the public, by an Anglo-Belgian dealer, Lambert Nieuwenhuys, on the first day of a sale in Paris of the collection of Monsieur Lapeyrière, a French inspector of taxes who was known to have a good eye for works of art. Nieuwenhuys paid 80,005 francs. His son, who was based in London, almost immediately offered it to the National Gallery for £3,800, while claiming that he had three other offers. This was the beginning of the growth of the collection, seizing opportunities as they arose and very often relying on dealers to act as intermediaries and bring works of art to the attention of the Trustees.

In 1826, the Chancellor of the Exchequer persuaded the House of Commons to vote £9,000 in order that the National Gallery could acquire a group of wonderful works from a bankrupt London jeweller, Thomas Hamlet – Titian's magnificent *Bacchus and Ariadne* (NG 35), still one of the greatest works in the collection and an obvious example of Grand Tour taste, Annibale Carracci's *Christ appearing to Saint Peter on the Appian Way* (NG 9) and Poussin's *A Bacchanalian Revel before a Term* (NG 62). A letter of recommendation was submitted by the Trustees and, in his speech in the House of Commons, Charles Long described how 'he knew of no other way in which purchases for the National Gallery could be so satisfactorily effected as by the recommendation of a committee of responsible persons'. This did not prevent the acquisition from being attacked in another letter to *The Times* claiming that the Trustees were not properly qualified. Long added slightly bitterly how 'With regard to the share which he himself had had in the formation of the National Gallery, he had found it rather an ungracious office. He was continually receiving letters, offering collections and sometimes single pictures for sale, and inviting him to call upon the possessors, and give his opinion as to their worth'.

The third great group of paintings which helped to establish the character of the National Gallery was the gift in 1831 of the Reverend William Holwell Carr. William Holwell (he had added Carr after his marriage) had studied at Exeter College, Oxford, become a Fellow, visited Italy, was an amateur painter, and, from 1791, the absentee rector of Menheniot in Cornwall. After marrying the daughter of the Earl of Errol in 1797, he could devote himself to collecting pictures as a dealer and, like so many of the people associated with the early history of the National Gallery, was a Director of the British Institution. He kept his collection in his house at 29, Devonshire Street, off Harley Street, where it was described by Prince Pückler-Muskau as 'the small private collection of a clergyman, which consists of not above 30 pictures, has cost him £20,000, and is quite worth it'. His gift to the National Gallery included Claude's *Landscape with David at the Cave of Adullam* (NG 6), Tintoretto's *St George and the Dragon* (NG 16), which had been in England since 1764, Guercino's *Dead Christ mourned by Two Angels* (NG 22) and Garofalo's *St Augustine with the Holy Family* (NG 81). This group of paintings reinforced the existing characteristics of the National Gallery's collection, being strong in Italian pictures of the sixteenth century, in works by Claude and Poussin, and including Rembrandt's *A Woman Bathing in a Stream* (NG 54), which Holwell Carr had bought for only 165 guineas at Lord Gwydir's sale in 1829.

Alongside the collection of Old Master paintings, the Trustees also acquired (or were given) representative examples of British art, which were expected to hang alongside the paintings by Old Masters in order to demonstrate the relationship between new work and old. Indeed, it requires a constant effort of imagination to remember that the National Gallery was not always simply a sanctuary of Old Master paintings, but was expected to include more modern, British work in order to provide an opportunity for comparison. John Julius Angerstein's collection included William Hogarth's *Self Portrait with a Pug*, alongside three paintings from Henry Fuseli's Milton Gallery and Wilkie's *The Village Holiday* (Tate Noo122). Considering his deep interest in contemporary art, George Beaumont owned fewer British paintings, but he had two important works by Richard Wilson, a *Distant View of Maecenas' Villa* (Tate Noo108) and *The Destruction of the Children of Niobe* (Yale Center for British Art B1977.14.81), which represented the way in which British painting had been influenced by Claude. Meanwhile, Charles Long presented Gainsborough's *The Watering Place* (NG 109) in

1827, having written to Henry Ellis how 'it appears to me very desirable that in the National Gallery of Painting, there should be included the Works of the most eminent Painters of the British School' and, in 1830, the Directors of the British Institution donated Reynolds' *Holy Family* (NG 79) and Gainsborough's *The Market Cart* (NG 80), which had been sold at Christie's in May 1829. The character of British paintings at the National Gallery has always been dominated by the classic painters of the late eighteenth century, by the work of Hogarth, Reynolds and Gainsborough, who were regarded as the best models for nineteenth-century art and whose work had been displayed in exhibitions at the British Institution, rather than by the works of artists such as Joseph Wright of Derby or Stubbs, who worked in the north of England, were more interested in genre, and whose style of painting was influenced by industrialisation.

In 1834, two Correggios, *Venus with Mercury and Cupid* (NG 10) and *Ecce Homo* (NG 15) were bought for £11,500 from the Marquess of Londonderry. Sir Robert Peel was Prime Minister, as well as a Trustee, and he suggested that the Trustees should seek the advice of experts besides Seguier, including Samuel Rogers, the bachelor poet and banker (shortly afterwards appointed a Trustee), and William Young Ottley, the Keeper of Prints and Drawings at the British Museum and a pioneer collector of early Italian painting (his house was described as 'covered from floor to ceiling with pictures by the old Pre-Raphaelite artists'). Queen Adelaide remarked that Londonderry had done well to sell these pictures – 'One is only suitable in a church. The other is certainly not suitable in a drawing room', a remark which suggests that the criteria of purchase for the National Gallery should be no different from those of a private collection.

In looking at the works of art which were acquired in the early years of the National Gallery, it is clear that, up until the mid-1830s, it would have been impossible to distinguish its collection from that of a rich, private collector. In 1835 an opportunity arose to buy early German pictures from the collection of the German businessman Carl Aders, which had been seen and admired by the Romantic poets, Coleridge and Wordsworth. Walter Savage Landor suggested that the entire collection should be acquired by the National Gallery and when the pictures were exhibited in Golden Square, the catalogue commented on the fact that 'neither the National Gallery, nor any of the Public Institutions contain speci-mens of the celebrated masterpieces of the old German and Flemish painters'. But when a copy of the Ghent Altarpiece was offered to Seguier, he replied that the Trustees 'had no funds and declined making any application to Government for works except for very extraordinary objects'.

The pictures were displayed in Angerstein's house in a fairly arbitrary way, hung floor-to-ceiling, without much sense of history or appropriate sequence. The first catalogue of the collection was published by Ottley in 1826 under the title *A descriptive catalogue of the pictures in the National Gallery with critical remarks on their merits*, and the second, *A descriptive, explanatory, and critical Catalogue of fifty of the earliest pictures contained in the National Gallery of Great Britain*, by John Landseer in 1834. As the Earl of Aberdeen, a Trustee, acknowledged in evidence to the 1853 Select Committee, the National Gallery looked 'merely like the collection of a private gentleman, and nothing more'.

### Planning a building
The National Gallery was originally housed in Angerstein's house which was a three-bay, domestic dwelling with a large room on the first floor where Sebastiano del Piombo's great *Raising of Lazarus* was displayed and a second floor upstairs for the British pictures. It was almost immediately

obvious that Angerstein's house was hopelessly inadequate as a long-term home for a national collection of paintings and particularly pathetic if compared to the Louvre.

So, when John Nash produced designs in 1825 (published in 1826) for the development of the space then occupied by William Kent's Royal Mews, now Trafalgar Square, he included a suggestion that the National Gallery should be placed on the north side of the square in a long, low building with domes and a Corinthian portico. In the middle of the square, he proposed a building designed in the form of a Greek or Roman temple to house the Royal Academy. He was perhaps inspired by the great drawings of the Roman Forum done by his nephew and pupil, James Pennethorne, in Rome and which were sent to Nash on 17 April 1825; or, alternatively, he may have been influenced in his conception of the building by the model of the Parthenon which he kept on the landing of the grand staircase of his house in Regent Street. On the east side of Trafalgar Square, Nash proposed a building for the Athenaeum Club and the Royal Academy of Literature. The west side was already earmarked for a building to house the College of Physicians and the Union Club, now Canada House, which was designed by Robert Smirke, the architect of the British Museum. In other words, Nash imagined the new Trafalgar Square as a central forum in the city for scholarly and public institutions, comparable in style and character to the designs which Hawksmoor had made, but not executed, more than a century earlier for Oxford and Cambridge.

As with so many of the schemes for the design of the National Gallery, some of these ideas had already been suggested at least twenty years before by James Wyatt who realised that the space occupied by the Royal Mews might provide an opportunity for a building which could house the national archives and the Royal Academy, as well as a National Gallery. In June 1828, a Select Committee suggested that the existing building could be adapted 'at a very small expense', a proposal which was endorsed by the Board of Trustees at a meeting held in the King's Mews on 15 July 1828 (it was only in 1828 that the Board began to meet at all regularly). In August, Nash was asked to produce a design for a new building. The *Literary Gazette* reported that Nash was 'to be entrusted with the erection of a National Gallery and a Royal Academy' and the *Gentleman's Magazine* that Nash's plans had obtained the necessary approval. Neither report was true. Instead, the Trustees began to investigate the possibility of buying the house immediately next door to Angerstein's house in Pall Mall in order to create a long frontage on Pall Mall, with space behind the two houses to allow for expansion. The British Institution advanced £4,000 towards the cost of this proposal, but the Duke of Wellington as Prime Minister 'would not listen to it'.

In 1830, when it was proposed that Angerstein's house should be demolished to make space for a road into St James's Square, the Board investigated an idea of constructing a new building on a vacant site immediately alongside St James's Palace, which had been available since a fire in 1809. In December 1830 the Trustees agreed the brief for a building which was to have consisted of three large, sky-lit galleries and rooms beneath for offices – in other words, nothing tremendously ambitious. But this idea also came to nothing.

In June 1831, Lord Dover, who, as Agar Ellis, had been one of the original proponents of a National Gallery in the House of Commons, in his capacity as the newly-appointed First Commissioner of Woods and Forests, inspected Dysart House in Pall Mall in order to consider it as a possible site for the National Gallery. It had the obvious attraction of relatively low costs of conversion. But, in August 1831, William Wilkins, the great Greek Revival architect, returned to the previous suggestion that the King's Mews should be adapted in such a way that it might house both the Royal Academy and the National Gallery. On 16 September 1831, the Trustees met at Lord Dover's house to consider Wilkins's proposals. They agreed that Angerstein's house was inadequate and that Wilkins's ideas provided the best possible, as well as the cheapest, solution. They wrote to the Prime Minister, Earl Grey, that the proposal was 'the most practicable that has hitherto been offered to them, and well adapted to that purpose' and, the following month, they showed Earl Grey the plans. According to Lord Dover, the Prime Minister 'seemed to like the plan – and promised to consider it favourably'.

Not long afterwards, on 20 November 1831, Wilkins published a short pamphlet entitled *A Letter to Lord Viscount Goderich on the Patronage of the Arts by the English Government* (Viscount Goderich had been the Chancellor of the Exchequer who had approved the funding of a National Gallery in February 1824). Wilkins compared the condition of the National Gallery in London to its equivalents on the continent and, in particular, noted the extreme inadequacy of Angerstein's house as a safe place in which to house a national collection:

> It is painful to witness the half measures adopted by the government in all its proceedings relating to the arts. The purchase of the Angerstein collection took place at a very favourable period, when public distress had not yet cramped their resources; still these fine and invaluable works have been suffered to remain in a mansion ill calculated for their display, and where they are subject at all times to the ravages of the elements. The principal room is above the Offices of the Keeper, where the accidental ignition of a chimney flue would subject the whole to immediate perdition.

He concluded that

> Whilst every nation on the continent, whether free or
> despotic, is engaged in the formation of galleries truly
> national, our own, the freest amongst the free, and . . .
> the most liberal in rewarding the production of native
> talent, have as yet pursued no such patriotic example.

In May 1832, a 'Committee of Gentlemen' was established
under Lord Duncannon, who had replaced Lord Dover as
First Commissioner of Woods and Forests, including Lord
Goderich, Lord Farnborough, Lord Dover, Sir Robert
Peel, Ridley Colborne, Samuel Rogers and Joseph Hume, a
Scottish merchant who became a radical MP, to consider the
whole question as to how best to house the National Gallery,
the Royal Academy, and the public records. Following the
new requirement that all public projects should be subject
to competition, three architects were then invited to submit
proposals: John Nash, at this point in his career well past
his prime, but an obvious choice as he had been responsible for so many of the major town planning projects in
London in the previous twenty years; C.R. Cockerell, who
had travelled widely in Italy and Greece and been responsible for Greek Revival country house commissions during
the 1820s; and William Wilkins, whose recent work had
included a number of gothic designs for Cambridge colleges
and a grand, Romanised temple front for the non-denomina-
tional University College, London.

Nash put forward a proposal for a long, colonnaded building, akin in character to his terraces round Regent's Park and
to the terraces along the Mall which replaced the demolished
Carlton House. But by now his ideas were probably regarded
as too scenographic – grand façades which looked effective as
part of a more general composition, but which often left much

to be desired in terms of their detailed planning and were felt to be lacking in intellectual, as well as physical, substance. Cockerell's magnificent proposals for a gallery 400 feet long over an arcade of shops (an early example of a public-private partnership) were regarded as too expensive. Wilkins's initial idea, on the other hand, was, as before, a matter of adapting the old Royal Mews building, originally designed by William Kent. It was on this basis that he was selected, as an architect who was prepared to undertake a relatively economical makeover of an existing building. It probably also helped that he was a close friend of Lord Aberdeen, one of the Trustees and a fellow student of archaeological remains.

However, by June 1832, the committee had become slightly more ambitious in its ideas and Wilkins was asked, instead, to put forward proposals for a free-standing building which would re-use the columns and entablature of Carlton House, the palace of the Prince Regent on the Mall which had recently been demolished.

Wilkins designed a building which was long and low, in some ways quite utilitarian and combining the functions of both gallery and academy into a single façade, facing south towards Whitehall and incorporating the National Gallery on its west side and the Royal Academy on its east. Many people both then and since have lamented the absence in his design of a proper sense of monumentality. It was as if he was trying to preserve some of the character and qualities of the previous Royal Mews, the shape of which, and, indeed, some aspects of the style of which, hover like a ghost behind Wilkins's design. But it is hard to reconstruct now the hostility which faced the building of every major project during this period of public works after the Napoleonic Wars: the determination to save public money at all costs, and the distaste for anything which might smack of *folie de grandeur.* Wilkins judged his clients correctly. There was just enough of a hint of grandeur in the central section of the façade, including the small, ultimately too insubstantial, dome. There was to be a certain amount of celebratory sculpture on the pediments, which was unexecuted in order to save money. And the reasons that made the design acceptable in the political circumstances of the early 1830s are precisely those that have won it affection, if not admiration, ever since. It lacks pomposity. It was not much different in style and character, nor, indeed, in cost to a moderately grand, Greek Revival country house. It was planned to cost £41,000 if built of brick and £10,000 more if stone.

Sir Robert Peel was an enthusiastic supporter of the scheme. He spoke in the House of Commons on 23 July 1832, advocating its broader social implications (it should be remembered that Peel was an opponent of the Great Reform Bill):

> In the present times of political excitement, the exacerbation of angry and unsocial feelings might be much softened by the effects which the fine arts had ever produced on the minds of men. Of all expenditure, that, like the present expenditure on a national gallery, is the most adequate to confer advantage on those classes which have but little leisure to enjoy the most refined species of pleasure. The rich may have their own pictures, but those who obtain their bread by their labour cannot hope for such enjoyment. The erection of the national gallery would not only contribute to the cultivation of the arts, but also to the cementing of the bonds of union between the richer and the poorer orders of the state.

By January 1833, Wilkins's design for the National Gallery was nearly complete. In order to protect the view of the façade of St Martin-in-the-Fields, the front had been set back

50 feet further north than Wilkins had originally planned. There had been a number of other changes. The subsidiary porticoes which led through to the barracks and workhouse behind had been moved forwards in order to try and give some sense of animation to what was otherwise always going to be an exceedingly long and slightly featureless façade. A semi-circular gallery had been added at the back. It was no longer felt necessary for the ground floor of the west wing to house the public records. And, as always seems to be the case with public projects, the costs had gone up, from £50,000 to £66,000, less £4,000 for the value of old materials from Carlton House, which could be sold.

The following month, Wilkins's scheme was leaked to the *Literary Gazette*. It was instantly the subject of intense public ridicule. What people realised right from the beginning was that the building was much too low for its setting, unable to dominate the space to the south. This was partly a consequence of its being designed to house not just one, but two great public institutions, the Royal Academy as well as the National Gallery: in other words, the portico was the only common element which united institutions whose rooms stretched out to either side. Moreover, public taste was already turning towards the idea of a richer and more monumental surface for public buildings and was much less in sympathy with the relative austerity of the Greek Revival, which had been pioneered and promoted by William Wilkins from Downing College in Cambridge onwards.

Colonel Sir Edward Cust, a vocal MP with a particular interest in public projects (he was the person who had insisted that any major public building project should be the subject of a competition), showed the engraving of Wilkins's building in the House of Commons alongside a Neo-Renaissance scheme which he had had drawn up by Charles Barry, who tended to prefer a more Italianate style to the neo-Greek, as is evident in the design of the Manchester Institution, now the Manchester City Art Gallery, and in the Travellers' Club, which had opened in 1829. Cust's purpose was to encourage the government to require Wilkins to make the design higher and more monumental.

On 25 April 1833, Wilkins wrote to Lord Duncannon, perhaps in response to public pressure, suggesting that the façade should, indeed, be raised by 5 feet, bringing it to the level of St Martin's and, at the same time, masking the roof of the Barracks behind. But, three days later, he argued against an increase of more than 5 feet on the grounds that it would interfere with the internal plan and diminish the quality of light in the top-lit picture galleries.

In May 1833, *The Times* suggested that the project should be moved altogether to Regent's Park in order to allow space for future extensions. And, in August, Lord Duncannon was forced to admit in the House of Commons that the costs had now risen to £70,000 and suggested that the whole scheme should be scrapped, Wilkins paid off, and the National Gallery moved to the Banqueting House in Whitehall.

Wilkins was, not surprisingly, devastated by the suggestion that his last great public project might be scrapped and wrote to Lord Duncannon: 'Your Lordship cannot be expected to be fully aware of this change of plans on my professional practice but I know it *must be* such as will leave me no option but that of retiring altogether from practice'. For whatever reason, this was a temporary glitch and, on 30 August 1833, the Treasury approved the scheme.

Wilkins's problems and difficulties were certainly not at an end. Many British public projects have suffered from being designed by committee, and because the Treasury has always wanted to save money and politicians to interfere. Nor was the design of the building exempt from changes during the course of construction. In particular, in June 1834, Wilkins was taken by Duncannon to see the sculptures which Nash had intended to use on Marble Arch. He was delighted to re-use them on the façade of the National Gallery. As he wrote to Duncannon, 'I am no advocate for the introduction of sculpture into buildings unless it be of excellent design and good execution', but he felt that these sculptures 'are of this description and may be made not only conducive to a certain degree of richness in the exterior but by breaking the horizontal <u>sky-line</u> greatly improve the general effect'. This is why you find over the front entrance of the National Gallery symbolic sculptures of Europe and Asia and an empty lunette which was originally intended to be filled with a commemorative bust of the Duke of Wellington which ended up inside the east entrance to the staff offices.

In July 1834, Wilkins realised that the idea of re-using the columns of Carlton House for the entrance portico was not going to work. To begin with, he thought that they could at least be used to embellish the side entrances; but, here too, he decided that, in the end, it was better to build new ones. He reported to Duncannon that he had

> engaged to erect both [gateways] of entirely new
> materials except the capitals of the columns, which have
> been wrought anew and have been made, by the removal
> of some of their ornamental foliage, to correspond
> with the greater simplicity of those intended to be
> introduced in the center portico of the buildings. By
> this arrangement I have been enabled to give a greater
> substance, as well as height, to the columns insomuch
> that the difference in bulk between them and the
> columns for the center portico will be imperceptible.

Although the workmen engaged on the project went on strike between August and October 1834 (strikes were not only a phenomenon of the twentieth century), the Royal Academy side of the building (i.e. the east side) was sufficiently complete for it to be used in 1836 for the display of the designs for the new Houses of Parliament. But already the public mood was beginning to turn against the project. In his *Contrasts* published in that year, Pugin used the new National Gallery, not yet open, as an example of all that was wrong with contemporary British architecture – too mean and utilitarian and lacking a proper historical sense of the Gothic. And at the hearings of the Select Committee on Arts and Manufactures, held in 1836, the number of pictures the gallery could show was compared very unfavourably to the Alte Pinakothek in Munich, which had the capacity for showing 1,600 pictures and, even more, the new Hermitage in St Petersburg, alongside the imperial palace, which could show at least 4,000.

By 1837, Wilkins was beginning to be worn out by the stresses and strains of the project. He urged the Office of Works to proceed with the levelling of Trafalgar Square and to allow for the construction of a terrace immediately in front of the new building. But he was convinced, probably rightly, that the Treasury had decided to torpedo this idea, and, on 26 May 1837, he informed the Commissioners of Woods and Forests, that he must let things take their course, for he had 'already suffered [him]self to be agitated to a degree prejudicial to [his] health if further prolonged'.

The building was finally available for inspection by Queen Victoria on 7 April 1838 and the National Gallery opened to the general public two days later. *The Times* greeted its opening as follows:

> The rooms . . . are but badly calculated for the purpose, and the interior of the plan is more than commensurate in defects with the absurdities and bad taste of the

outside . . . It is distressing to see the manner in which
the pictures are hid in little receptacles.

Thackeray, meanwhile, dismissed the building as 'a little
gin-shop', while King William IV is said to have described it
just before his death, in his last recorded utterance, as 'a nasty
little pokey hole'. Compared to the grandeur of Schinkel's
Altes Museum in Berlin or Leo von Klenze's Alte Pinakothek
in Munich with its huge, top-lit galleries and side-lit cabinet
rooms, let alone the staggering opulence of Klenze's designs
for a purpose-built museum wing added to the Hermitage
in St Petersburg in 1839, Britain had acquired a National
Gallery which was relatively utilitarian and lacking adequate
space for expansion. From this point onwards, most of the
efforts of all subsequent building projects at the National
Gallery have been intended to correct, as far as possible, the
defects of William Wilkins's original design.

## A more historical approach

From the foundation of the National Gallery, there were calls
for the collection to be displayed historically, rather than
aesthetically, most persuasively in a passage (which he later
suppressed) of Disraeli's novel, *Vivien Grey*, published in
1826:

> We are now forming, at great expense, and with great
> anxiety, a National Gallery. What is the principal
> object of such an Institution? Doubtless to elevate
> the productions of our own school, by affording our
> artists an opportunity of becoming acquainted with the
> works of the great masters who have preceded them.
> Why, then have we deviated from the course which has
> been pursued in the formation of all other National
> Galleries? There we shall see arranged in chronological

order, specimens of the art in all ages, from the period
in which Cimabue rescued it from the Greek painters,
unto the present time.

The implication of this passage is clear: that if one looked
at galleries on the continent, then they were displayed much
more historically than the relatively haphazard displays in
Angerstein's house in Pall Mall – as 'specimens' using the
language of natural history. This was certainly the case with
the Berlin Altes Museum, which opened in 1830 in a building
designed by Karl Friedrich Schinkel and contained pictures
from all the schools of European painting, with a detailed
catalogue arranged according to national schools by its
extremely scholarly Director, Gustav Waagen.

In July 1835, the Select Committee on Arts and their
Connexion with Manufactures heard evidence from Waagen,
who made the case for collecting earlier works on the grounds
that 'the works of such masters have great influence in forming the taste in the best manner, and in inculcating the best
principles of art'. He argued that 'in order to understand and
still better appreciate the great masters, you must commence
with those who immediately preceded them and who taught
them'. This was clearly a much more historical and academic
approach to the task of collecting, reinforced by the evidence
of Edward Solly, one of a family of Baltic timber merchants
in London, who, during his travels, particularly in Germany,
had become a collector of early Italian, early German and
Flemish paintings, which he had sold to the Prussian state in
1821. He stated that 'there has not been sufficient attention
paid to extending of the collection' and that, if it was to be
'a complete historical collection . . . it must commence from
the time of Giotto'.

Solly was especially scathing about the qualifications
of the Trustees, whom he regarded as 'gentlemen of taste,

but I am not aware that they are gentlemen possessing the knowledge which, it appears to me, is requisite to be good judges of the ancient masters, and to point out what pictures would be desirable'. It was true that the Trustees were generally amateurs, with an educated, but essentially unacademic, knowledge of the history of art and Solly compared them unfavourably to the Committee responsible for purchases at the Royal Gallery in Berlin, which was 'composed partly of professors of painting, of the directors of the gallery (including the Gallery restorer), of other persons who, without being artists, have made the knowledge of pictures their study'. Poor Seguier, the Keeper, was forced to admit that he was not aware of 'any plan (proposed by the Trustees) for collecting the best specimens of the old masters'.

These discussions in the 1835 Select Committee are the first clear evidence of a future conflict in ideas and attitudes between the Trustees who have tended very much to guard their amateur status and to believe that they are the best judges of art, as a result of their upbringing and because they have often been collectors themselves, and the professional staff of the National Gallery, who have normally wanted the collection to be used for purposes of study and so have adopted a more historical and academic approach. As the collecting of works of art became more professional during the 1830s, there was a move away from the rather random and eclectic choice of Old Masters, acquired as opportunity arose, to a more systematic approach. This change was perhaps evident in the purchase of Raphael's *Saint Catherine* (NG 168), acquired in 1839 from William Beckford on the recommendation of Baron Christian Carl Josias Bunsen, who was a friend of Waagen and had a particular interest in Raphael.

In 1842, influenced by the increasing interest in art of the low countries and by the beginnings of the Gothic Revival, the Trustees were able to acquire Jan van Eyck's *Arnolfini*

*Portrait* (NG 186), one of the greatest works in the collection, which, owing to 'its perfect preservation, its extreme rarity and the moderate price at which it may now be obtained, viz. 600 guineas, induce [the Trustees] to recommend it without hesitation'. The acquisition of the *Arnolfini Portrait* marks a shift away from Grand Tour taste towards an interest in the early masters. It was to be a picture which was to be as important to the Pre-Raphaelites with their interest in microscopic precision of pictorial technique as Poussin and Claude had been to the artists and landscape gardeners of the late eighteenth century.

By now the new building was open. The first gallery one entered was the so-called 'Great Room', painted olive green, up the steep staircase to the left of Wilkins's entrance vestibule. Following the example of Angerstein's main room in his house in Pall Mall, it displayed Sebastiano's *Raising of Lazarus*, together with Titian's *Bacchus and Ariadne*, Parmigianino's *Vision of St Jerome*, and Correggio's *Mercury instructing Cupid before Venus*. There was still no attempt to provide a consistent historical or geographical sequence, because the room also included Murillo's *The Two Trinities*, a group of Claudes, and two works by Gaspard Poussin. The pictures were double hung, further hindering a clear narrative, as well as being tilted slightly forward in order to prevent dust gathering on their surface.

Nonetheless, according to Colonel Thwaites, the Assistant Keeper, giving evidence before the Select Committee in 1841, the paintings were 'arranged as nearly as possible according to the schools, that is, the Great-room entirely filled with Italian pictures, the next largest room is all Flemish (i.e. Netherlandish), with a few of the superfluity of Italian pictures; the third room is filled again with some inferior Italian pictures and some new acquisitions of Italian pictures and English pictures'. But the Gallery as a whole was regarded by informed observers as being shabby, like 'an ill-regulated workhouse', in contrast to the splendour of Leo von Klenze's Alte Pinakothek in Munich.

In 1843, Henry Cole, the civil-servant-cum-journalist who later became Director of the Victoria and Albert Museum, published his pseudonymous guide under the title *Felix Summerly's Hand-Book for the National Gallery* and, in the following year, George Foggo, a portrait painter who had studied at the École des Beaux-Arts in Paris, published *The National Gallery: its Pictures and their Painters, with Critical Remarks*, which ran into several editions. These were attempts to make the collection intelligible to the public. In the same year, Anna Jameson published her *Companion to the Most celebrated Private Galleries of Art in London*, which specifically recommended that 'A public gallery should be arranged with a view to instruction' and, in a letter to *The Times* published in 1847, John Ruskin, newly famous after the publication of *Modern Painters*, wrote to complain about the muddle of the hang and suggested that 'Every gallery should be long enough to admit of its whole collection being hung in one line, side by side, and wide enough to allow of the spectators retiring to the distance at which the largest picture was intended to be seen'. He also suggested that drawings and engravings should be shown alongside the paintings.

This passage indicates the way in which the opening of the new building and the opportunity for a wider public to see the collection stimulated public debate about what were the best conditions for viewing paintings, so that they might be hung in a logical sequence, in contrast to the old tradition of the salon, in which spectators were expected to make their own interpretation.

# 3. CHARLES EASTLAKE
## 1843–7

Following the death of William Seguier on 5 November 1843, Robert Peel appointed a member of the Royal Academy, Charles Eastlake, as his successor.(Since Eastlake is one of the great heroes in the history of the National Gallery, it is worth describing the formation of his taste.)

Born in 1793, educated at Plymouth Grammar School and at Charterhouse, Eastlake had been trained as a painter at the Royal Academy Schools. In 1815, he travelled to France and was inspired by the paintings which had been looted from foreign collections and displayed in the great galleries of the Musée Napoléon in the Louvre. Partly as a result of this experience, he acquired an unusually intense interest in the history of art. He then travelled to Rome where, after exploring Naples and travelling to Athens, he set himself up in a studio at 12 Piazza Mignanelli. He stayed for fourteen years. During his years in Italy, he acquired an infinitely broader and deeper knowledge of art than the great majority of his British contemporaries with an earnest and rather academic knowledge of the historical practice of art. As well as being friendly with two important young architects, Charles Barry and C.R. Cockerell, he also knew a number of contemporary German artists, including Baron von Rumohr and Johann David Passavant, who were themselves fascinated by the history of art (Passavant was a student of Raphael) and were associated with the group known as the Nazarenes, who modelled their style on early Italian art.

In 1828, after briefly returning to England where he had made his reputation as a painter of scenes of Italian *banditti*,

Eastlake travelled for nearly three months in Flanders, the Netherlands, Germany, and northern Italy, studying works of art in the newly established museums and galleries on the continent and buying books for his library.

So, when Eastlake was appointed Keeper of the National Gallery in 1843, he was a completely different kind of person from Seguier. He was a well-established scholar of art. He had translated Goethe's *Theory of Colours* in 1840 and F.T. Kugler's widely read book on the Italian schools of painting in 1842. The move from Seguier to Eastlake was essentially the move from the Regency to the Victorian age: from smart amateurism to professional dedication, from the world of the picture dealer and restorer to that of the scholar and art historian.

Eastlake immediately embarked on an adventurous programme of acquisitions. On 22 April 1844, he bought Giovanni Bellini's magnificently impassive portrait of *Doge Leonardo Loredan* (NG 189) from William Beckford's collection, an acquisition which was rightly praised by *The Athenaeum* as demonstrating 'our assurance of what Mr. Eastlake's conservatorship would attempt (and, we trust, accomplish) towards elevating and purifying popular taste, through the influence of its preparatory school'. In May 1844, he persuaded Robert Peel to allow a sum of £3,000 so that the Gallery could bid at Christie's sale of Jeremiah Harman's paintings (Harman had been one of Eastlake's patrons). John Seguier, William Seguier's brother, bid on the Gallery's behalf and acquired Gerrit Dou's *Portrait of a Man* (NG 192), then regarded as a self-portrait, and Guido Reni's *Jesus and St John* (NG 191). Immediately after the sale, the Gallery was able to acquire Rembrandt's *A Bearded Man in a Cap* (NG 190) by paying a 10 per cent premium.

On 13 May 1844, Peel wrote to Eastlake warning him of the perils of buying works according to their art-historical significance, rather than their intrinsic merit, suggesting that there may still have been a view amongst the Trustees that Eastlake was too academic in his taste. Peel argued that the National Gallery 'should give preference to works of sterling merit . . . rather than purchase curiosities in painting valuable certainly as illustrating the progress of art, or the distinctions in the styles of different masters, but surely less valuable than works approaching to perfection'. His comments are an indication of the continuing fault-line between the Trustees wishing to make acquisitions according to their eye and judgment and the more art-historical interests of the Director and his staff.

In July 1844, Eastlake was able to acquire Rubens's *The Judgment of Paris* (NG 194) for 4,000 guineas and Guido Reni's *Lot and his Daughters leaving Sodom* (NG 193) in the same sale for £1,680. The purchase of another Reni infuriated Ruskin, who wrote to his friend Henry Liddell, the Greek lexicographer and father of Alice in Wonderland, to complain about Eastlake's preference for a Baroque painter instead of buying the Quattrocento works which Ruskin would have liked him to acquire: 'It puts me into a desperate rage when I hear of Eastlake's buying Guidos for the National Gallery. He at least should know better – not that I anticipate anything looking at his art, but from his reputed character and knowledge.'

In early 1845, Eastlake tried to persuade the Trustees to buy Michelangelo's unfinished *Madonna and Child with St John and the Angels* (NG 809), but, failing this, encouraged them to buy a picture which he believed to be by Holbein (NG 195) and had a false inscription as such, but which, when hung in the Gallery in June, led to a widespread public outcry, owing to legitimate doubts as to its attribution.

Eastlake was at the same time preoccupied by the problems of the building, publishing *Observations on the unfitness of the present building for its purpose in a letter to Sir Robert Peel.* He was interested in all aspects of the heating, lighting and ventilation of galleries and believed that the system of display needed to be improved. In particular, he was worried about the skylights which allowed soot into the building, suggested that the National Gallery might be better located in the suburbs, and commented on the appropriate background against which to hang paintings:

> Pictures, considered as hangings for walls, have unquestionably the effect of darkening a room, and hence it may be desirable to counteract this effect by the lightest grounds. Such rooms require to be less illuminated at night; and thus the evil of a multitude of lights, which have the effect of vitiating and heating the air, is, in some degree, avoided.

Peel, on the other hand, thought that St James's Palace would provide a better site for a new building and commissioned James Pennethorne as surveyor of the crown estate to draw up plans both for a new building and for a new picture gallery and sculpture room at the back of the Wilkins building. Nothing came of either suggestion following Peel's fall from power in 1846.

During 1846 there was a great rumpus over Eastlake's policy of cleaning pictures, the first time that the public was to feel that the Gallery's authorities were too radically interventionist in the way they looked after works of art. When Charles Eastlake had been appointed Keeper in 1843, he apparently found the pictures in very poor condition and so consulted John Seguier as to what should be done. The Trustees agreed that the dirtiest pictures might be cleaned while the Gallery was closed in September and October 1846. Whatever was done – probably nothing more than a light cleaning with soap and water and spirits of wine (this was the normal procedure of the time) – led to virulent public opposition. The public liked their pictures dirty. A splenetic artist-turned-picture dealer, Morris Moore, who had fought in the Greek War of Independence and shared a studio with Alfred Stevens in Rome, sent a series of letters to *The Times* under the pseudonym 'Verax' in which he accused Eastlake of having 'flayed' the nation's paintings. He wrote

> I found the finest Rubens we possess completely flayed
> . . . With characteristic ignorance the fine rich glazings
> have been scoured off without the slightest regard
> to perception or proportion, so that we have distant
> objects most offensively confusing themselves with those
> in the foreground.

In a subsequent letter he added that Titian's *Bacchus and Ariadne* 'had been scraped raw in some parts' and 'repainted in others'.

In vain did Eastlake defend the cleaning to his Trustees on the grounds that Rubens's *Peace and War* (NG 46) 'may be said to have been long buried under repeated coats of yellowed and soiled varnish'. By December 1846, William Coningham, a Radical MP and collector of what the *Art Union* described as 'the faded and soul-less attempts at painting of the thirteenth and fourteenth centuries', had joined the attack. He published his letters under the title, *Picture Cleaning in the National Gallery with some Observations on the Royal Academy*. He agreed that the Rubens 'had been skinned' and added a gratuitous criticism of Eastlake's expertise:

> Can Sir Robert Peel be in earnest in speaking of Mr
> Eastlake's consummate knowledge of art? Is it in
> consequence of the purchase of 'the libel on Holbein'

and of the spurious Guido, or the edition of Kugler's *Handbook of Painting*, one of the most unsound works upon art with which I am acquainted, that we are called upon to suspend our judgment on the cleaning of pictures in the National Gallery?

John Ruskin put the argument for the Rubens having been damaged most cogently in a letter to *The Times*:

> I have no hesitation in asserting that for the present it is utterly and for ever partially destroyed. I am not disposed lightly to impugn the judgment of Mr. Eastlake, but this was indisputably of all the pictures in the gallery that which least required and least could endure the process of cleaning. It was in the most advantageous condition under which a work of Rubens can be seen; mellowed by time into more perfect harmony than when it left the easel, enriched and warmed without losing any of its freshness . . .

Although exonerated from criticism by his Trustees, Eastlake not long afterwards resigned from the post of Keeper in order to be able to concentrate on writing and research, which had led to the publication of his great scholarly monograph, still in print, *Materials for a History of Oil Painting*, and on his duties, equally onerous, as Secretary of the recently established Royal Fine Arts Commission.

# 4. THOMAS UWINS
## 1847-55

Eastlake's successor was Thomas Uwins, who had been born on 24 February 1782, trained as an engraver under Benjamin Smith, and then, like Eastlake, in the Royal Academy Schools. He worked as a miniaturist and watercolour painter until his bad eyesight compelled him to travel to Rome, where he became a friend of Eastlake. When he returned to London, he was appointed librarian of the Royal Academy and surveyor of Queen Victoria's pictures (he was responsible for the first *catalogue raisonné* of the Royal collection). He described himself when in Italy as 'a little meagre swarthy figure', was remembered as completely bald, and had a fairly wretched time as Keeper of the National Gallery, twice grilled by parliamentary Select Committees for its failings and widely regarded as someone who should have been fired.

Uwins's period as Keeper coincided with a period when there was an extremely lively public debate in parliament, in books and in periodicals as to how the National Gallery should operate, who its audience should be, and where it should be located. This was the period when ideas and beliefs about the National Gallery changed from it being treated as a gentleman's club to a much broader and more democratic set of beliefs about its audience, represented most obviously by the writings of Ruskin and Charles Kingsley, who, in a much-quoted essay on the National Gallery, described how

> picture-galleries should be the townsman's paradise of refreshment . . . There, in the space of a single room, the townsman may take his country walk – a walk beneath

mountain peaks, blushing sunsets, with broad woodlands spreading out below it: a walk through green meadows, under cool mellow shades, and overhanging rocks, by rushing brooks, where he watches and watches till he seems to *hear* the foam whisper, and to *see* the fishes leap; and his hard-worn heart wanders out free, beyond the grimy city-world of stone and iron, smoky chimneys, and roaring wheels, into the world of beautiful things.

Uwins's first duty was to deal with the offer of a group of early Italian paintings owned by the dealer, Samuel Woodburn, who had premises nearby at 112, St Martin's Lane and who had assisted Sir Thomas Lawrence with the acquisition of Old Master drawings. The proposed gift would have included a substantial group of drawings and of paintings intended to show the evolution of European art. The Trustees turned the offer down, so Woodburn threatened to make the same offer to the University of Oxford. On the other hand, the Trustees did accept a gift of early Italian paintings, including two sections of an altarpiece showing *Adoring Saints* by Lorenzo Monaco (NG 215–16), from William Coningham, the author of the attack on the National Gallery's cleaning policies, who had acquired them in Italy as by Taddeo Gaddi.

The other important gift which Uwins had to deal with was of the Vernon Collection, a miscellaneous collection of mainly Victorian narrative pictures, but which included Turner's *The Dogana, S Giorgio, Citella, from the Steps of the Dogana* (Tate N00372), the first Turner to enter the collection, and some eighteenth-century paintings, including Reynolds' *Self-portrait* (Tate N00306). It could not easily be housed in the existing building, so, to begin with, they were hung in the basement rooms on the ground floor, before being shipped off in 1850 to Marlborough House on the Mall and, then, in 1859 to the South Kensington Museum, where they were shown alongside the Sheepshanks Collection in a display of modern British art. The gift led to a Select Committee being established in 1848 to look into the issue of how best to house the National Gallery now that it had already so obviously outgrown its existing accommodation.

Charles Barry reported to the Select Committee that, in his view, the 'great defect of the present building' was its 'lowness and its broken outline, by which is produced both a want of unity and dignity' and Charles Eastlake, no longer Keeper, commented on the 'rather bald and frigid effect' of the interiors, whose walls did 'not correspond with the preciousness which the spectator attaches to the pictures'. The committee recommended that Pennethorne's plans for a new building at the back of the Wilkins building should be shelved, the Royal Academy turned out of the west end of the building, and that the gallery should be completely rebuilt on the Trafalgar Square site. According to Eastlake, this would at last make possible 'the great purpose for which the National Gallery is supposed to be established; that of forming a complete collection relating to the history of the art, and to exhibit the pictures that are collected so as to benefit those who are to study them'.

In March 1850, the Prime Minister, Lord John Russell announced in the House of Commons that the Royal Academy was going to move from Trafalgar Square and Pennethorne published plans which would have transformed the two sequences of rooms of the Wilkins building (the one to the west for the National Gallery and the one to the east for the Royal Academy) into a long gallery following the model of the Alte Pinakothek in Munich and of the Galeries de Batailles at Versailles. At the back of the building, he wanted to build an ambitious extension, which was expected to display not only sculpture from the British Museum, but also Mantegna's great canvases of the *Triumphs of Caesar*, acquired by Charles I and now at Hampton Court, and to include a major art library, where students would have been free to study the history of art in a way which was only made possible later in the South Kensington Museum.

Again, nothing came of these proposals and, in June 1850, another Select Committee was established 'to consider the present accommodation afforded by the National Gallery'. It consisted of many of the same people as in 1848, but, on this occasion, it recommended that the National Gallery should move away from Trafalgar Square altogether.

One of the problems evident during Uwins's time was that the National Gallery had become a victim of its own success. It was preoccupied by the issue of overcrowding and, also, by the sorts of people who were attracted to the Gallery and how they were using it.

In his evidence to the various Committees, Uwins provided graphic descriptions of visitors and of how 'on one occasion, I saw a school of boys, imagine 20, taking their satchels from their backs with their bread and cheese, sitting down and making themselves very comfortable, and eating their luncheon' and 'on another occasion, I saw some people, who seemed to be country people, who had a basket of provisions, and who drew their chairs round and sat down, and seemed to make themselves very comfortable; they had meat and drink; and when I suggested to them the impropriety of such a proceeding in such a place, they were very good-humoured, and a lady offered me a glass of gin'. In their Report, the 1850 Commissioners recorded how

> It appears that the Gallery is frequently crowded by
> large masses of people, consisting not merely of those
> who come for the purpose of seeing the pictures, but
> also of persons having obviously for their object the
> use of the rooms for wholly different purposes; either
> for shelter in case of bad weather, or a place in which

children of all ages may exercise and play, and not
infrequently as one where food and refreshments may
conveniently be taken.

In 1853, the artist William Dyce published a report on *The
National Gallery: its Formation and Management* as a letter
addressed to Prince Albert. He argued that the collection
ought properly to provide an overview of the development of
art encompassing all periods, particularly the so-called 'early
Christian' (by which he meant work of the fourteenth and fifteenth centuries), in which he discerned 'freshness of thought
and intention, a vivacity, a gaiety, a vividness of impression'.
As a result of this Report, the government established yet
another Select Committee 'To inquire into the management of
the National Gallery; also to consider in what mode the col-
lective monuments of antiquity and fine art possessed by the
nation may be most securely preserved, judiciously augmented,
and advantageously exhibited to the public'. It was chaired by
Colonel Richard Mure, Conservative MP for Renfrewshire.

In its Report, the 1853 Select Committee produced a series
of recommendations, above all that the Gallery needed a new
system of management including a Director with appropriate
authority to make acquisitions and expected, as suggested
by Eastlake, to act 'with discretion and discrimination',
together with a proper acquisitions policy if it was ever to
rival the major galleries on the continent, particularly those in
Germany. Its conclusion was that 'What Chaucer and Spenser
are to Shakespeare and Milton – Giotto and Masaccio are to
the great masters of the Florentine School; and a National
Gallery would be as defective without adequate specimens of
both styles of painting, as a National Library without specimens of both styles of poetry'.

Not long afterwards, Pennethorne proposed that the
National Gallery should go either to the site now occupied by

the Albert Memorial on Kensington Gore or, alternatively, just south of the Round Pond in Kensington Gardens. Again, nothing was done about the proposals and the only change to the National Gallery was to its decoration, including a swing door to help keep out the smog and a new colour scheme, described by the Keeper, Thomas Uwins:

> It may be remembered that the colour of the walls was a repulsive and ineffective cold grey green; for this has been very judiciously substituted a dark red paper, embossed, but the pattern is not so prominent as in any wise to importune the eye.

In 1854, after a period of absolute chaos in the affairs of the Gallery and after Gladstone as Chancellor of the Exchequer had persuaded the Trustees to buy sixty-four early German pictures from the Krüger collection, of which a large percentage were regarded as of dubious attribution (only seventeen now remain in the collection), it became clear that the system of management needed to be reformed, that authority should be vested in a newly appointed Director, and that the Keeper, Thomas Uwins, should retire. The Prime Minister, Lord Aberdeen, first offered the post to an art historian, James Dennistoun, who turned it down on the grounds that no one in their right mind would want to accept a post which involves 'endless squabbling from bigwigs and blackguards for some 600 or 800 pounds a year'. Encouraged by the Queen and Prince Albert, Aberdeen then appointed Eastlake not as Keeper, but, for the first time, as a fully-fledged Director with the appropriate level of authority to run the institution – under but, to a substantial extent, free from interference from his Board of Trustees. The press was deeply critical, regarding it as a court appointment and 'a national disgrace'. But the press was wrong.

# 5. SIR CHARLES EASTLAKE
## 1855–65

The appointment of Eastlake as Director led to a much more professional approach not only to the collection of works of art, but also to their study. Not only was Eastlake an extremely worldly and well-connected public figure as President of the Royal Academy, with his reputation as an administrator enhanced by service on the committee of the Great Exhibition, but he also had a meticulous, scholarly temperament, used to the minute study of works of art and to the description of the characteristics of their style in the notebooks which he kept on his travels. He was the right person at the right moment to fortify the collections of the National Gallery with wide-ranging acquisitions, travelling during the late summer and autumn round Italy, staying in the *palazzi* of impoverished Italian nobles, and able to buy works of art with relative freedom.

The *Treasury Minute, dated 27 March 1855, Reconstituting the Establishment of the National Gallery* described how

> The selection of pictures must, of course, be left in a great measure to the judgment of the Director, aided by the Trustees, but my Lords are of the opinion that, as a general rule, preference should be given to fine pictures for sale abroad. As regards the finer works of art in this country, it may be assumed that, although they may change hands, they will not leave our shores, whereas the introduction of fine works from abroad would form a positive addition to the treasures of art in England. My Lords are also of the opinion that,

as a general rule, preference should be given to good
specimens of the Italian schools, including those of the
earlier masters.

It is interesting to see the extent to which it was understood
at the time that by far the best way to improve the quality and
character of the collection was to acquire works of art overseas and to give the Director both the freedom and the funds
to secure them. Equally, it was presumed at this time that the
landowners who had acquired so many works of art for their
private collections during the previous hundred years were
unlikely to want to sell them, a situation which only began to
change in the 1880s.

The Treasury Minute limited the role of the Trustees as
being simply 'to keep up a connexion between the cultivated
lovers of art and the institution, to give their weight and aid,
as public men, on many questions in art of a public nature
that may arise, and to form an indirect though useful channel
of communication between the government of the day and
the institution'. This is a very good and clear description of
the appropriate balance of authority and meant that, at last,
there was an effective Director with Eastlake in charge. The
terms of his appointment also included a requirement that

> One of the most important duties of the Director, and
> one which will require great care and attention, will
> be to construct a correct history of every picture in
> the collection, including its repairs, and describing
> accurately its present condition, which history will be
> continued from time to time by new entries as occasion
> may require.

At the same time that Eastlake was appointed as Director,
aged sixty-two, so too was Ralph Wornum, an art critic, as

Keeper on a salary on £750 a year. He had nearly as good a knowledge of the history of art as Eastlake, having spent six years studying abroad in museums and galleries in the 1830s, published an *Outline of a General History of Painting amongst the Ancients* in 1847, and been the author of the first official catalogue of the National Gallery's collection under Eastlake's supervision. He was described by W.S. Spanton, who was a Royal Academy student, as 'a big stout man, with perfectly straight white hair, deep lines in his forehead, and a slightly irritable manner'. Otto Mündler, a Bavarian picture dealer who had travelled widely on the continent and was the author of a recent essay on the Italian pictures in the Louvre in which he criticised the Director for failings of attribution, was hired as travelling agent to scout for pictures overseas, with a salary of £300 a year and £600 for travelling expenses.

Together these three completely transformed the National Gallery's fortunes. It now had a professional and knowledgeable staff, able to recommend acquisitions to the Trustees and an adequate purchase grant of £10,000 a year. The National Gallery was transformed from an amateur operation into a professional one and a monument to high Victorian intellectual, scholarly and artistic ambition.

In August 1855, Charles Eastlake set off on the first of his annual continental journeys with his wife, Elizabeth, herself a formidable scholar and author of numerous works of art history, including a translation of J.D. Passavant's essay on English art collections under the title *A Tour of a German Artist in England*. They met up with Otto Mündler in Paris and toured in France, Germany and Italy, studying museums and private collections.

During September 1855, Eastlake was able to buy Botticelli's tondo of the *Virgin and Child, St John and two Angels* (NG 226) (it is now regarded as by Botticelli's workshop) from a British banker, Benozzo Gozzoli's *Virgin and Child Enthroned* (NG 283) from the Rinuccini estate, and another Botticelli tondo, the *Virgin and Child, St John and the Angel* (NG 275) from the Bianconi collection in Bologna. One can see immediately that he was prepared to buy aggressively in the area of fifteenth-century Italian painting, particularly works by Botticelli, which had not hitherto been at all well represented in the collection, but appealed to Victorian religious taste. Lady Eastlake described the negotiations in a letter to her mother

> My dear husband is (between ourselves) in full treaty
> for some prizes and has more prospect of getting what
> is really grand and fine than we could have expected.
> But this requires much patience, prudence and caution.
> We are taken to one palace after another . . . most of the
> owners are needy and in debt; and now these late Paris
> fêtes are likely to play into our hands, for the Dukes are
> returning home with more than empty pockets and glad
> to have good prices for things which, in their opinion,
> any modern daub will replace.

On his return to London in late October, Eastlake was able to report to the Trustees how 'I have made an offer for a Mantegna now in the possession of the Somaglia family of Milan. The ultimate sum proposed for this work was 40,000 francs (about £1,600). The negotiation has been entrusted to a confidential agent in Milan and it is probable that the picture may be obtained for a less sum'. This was Mantegna's altarpiece, the *Virgin and Child between the Magdalen and S. John the Baptist* (NG 274), which was acquired by Mündler from the dealer, Roverselli, in Milan, in December 1855, for £1,125-12s. In November, Eastlake also acquired Veronese's enormous *Adoration of the Kings* (NG 268), from a dealer, Angelo Toffoli, an acquisition which was much criticised in parliament on the grounds that it was regarded as studio work.

In December 1856, Mündler was able to negotiate the purchase of ten pictures from Baron Galvagna, a previous President of the Accademia delle Belle Arti in Venice, including Giovanni Bellini's *Virgin and Child (Madonna of the Pomegranate)* (NG 280). Again, it is clear that Eastlake's taste was for the Quattrocento, buying works of art at a time when they were freely available and could be exported to England without too much difficulty. As Lady Eastlake wrote, describing what she saw as the situation of works of art in Italy in her characteristically forthright style (she was known jokingly as 'Lago Maggiore' because of her girth), 'They are so shamefully indifferent here about the preservation of their works of art, that the most glorious things are allowed to perish from sheer contempt and ill-treatment . . . the most precious specimens are dying a lingering death in their filthy churches'.

In 1856, Eastlake was fortunate in receiving a bequest, which included Titian's *Noli Me Tangere* (NG 270), from Samuel Rogers, a poet, collector and friend of Byron and Shelley, who had been a Trustee and whose house at 22, St James's Place was so stuffed with pictures, engravings, antiquities, books, and furniture, that, according to Byron, 'There is not a gem, a coin, a book, thrown aside on his chimney piece, his sofa, his table, that does not bespeak an almost fastidious elegance in the possessor'. He also acquired *Two Haloed Mourners* (NG 276), a fresco fragment by Spinello Aretino, but which was then attributed to Giotto, for £78 from Rogers's collection when it was sold at Christie's on 2–3 May 1856.

In June 1856, Mündler embarked on negotiations to buy Veronese's enormous, stately painting of *The Family of Darius before Alexander* (NG 294), one of the greatest works in the National Gallery's collection. He was assisted by the British Vice-Consul in Venice and by the promise of a separate purchase grant from parliament. On 4 March 1857, its owner, Conte Vittore Pisani, set extremely tough terms for the purchase. It was to cost £12,280, minus its frame. The money was to be paid in silver. He also required tips for his staff. As soon as the money had been paid, Pisani's responsibilities were to end, irrespective of any difficulties in obtaining an export licence. It was a major acquisition, but its cost, more than the annual purchase grant, caused uproar in parliament, led by Lord Elcho, who was particularly enraged by the payments to the Count's servants, and it resulted in the dismissal of Mündler in spite of the fact that Lord Palmerston criticised the House of Commons for 'haggling and boggling about a paltry sum'. As Joseph Crowe, the art historian who had recently returned from covering the Crimean War for the *Illustrated London News*, wrote:

> Parliament has refused to sanction a continuance of Mündler's appointment. And why? Because, after difficult and prolonged negotiations, he had succeeded in enriching the National Collection with the great 'Alexander and the Family of Darius' by Paolo Veronese, a monumental work which is one of the painter's masterpieces, and, according to Mr. Ruskin, 'the most precious Paolo Veronese in the world'.

Later in 1856, Eastlake had to deal with the consequences of the settlement of the Turner Bequest. J.M.W. Turner had died in 1851 leaving approximately 100 finished paintings, 182 unfinished, nearly 20,000 drawings and sketches, and two paintings, *Dido building Carthage* (NG 498) and *Sun rising through Vapour* (NG 479), which he had specified were to be hung alongside two Claudes in the collection, the *Seaport* and the *Mill*, which he had known and loved ever since they had been bought by Angerstein. But, as with the Vernon Collection, the National Gallery did not have space for the Turner Bequest and, like the Vernon Collection, the Turners were initially shown in Marlborough House, until the Trustees realised that Turner's will required that the collection was to be shown in purpose-built rooms in the National Gallery.

Eastlake's major acquisition in 1857 was Pollaiuolo's large altarpiece, the *Martyrdom of St Sebastian* (NG 292), another great work of the Quattrocento, demonstrating Eastlake's taste for pictures, both from Florence and northern Italy, which were influenced by an interest in the antique. He had first seen the picture in Florence in 1855, but the owner, Marchese Roberto Pucci, was then asking £6,000 for it. Eastlake admired it as 'one of the earliest extant, and certainly the most important example of the art of oil painting, as that art, adopted from the Flemish Masters, was practised in Florence . . . and also that many critics considered this painting as one of the first that stimulated Florentine painters to a study of anatomy'. By 1857, the Marchese had indicated that he was willing to sell the painting for around £3,000 and Eastlake managed to acquire it for £3,155. There were difficulties over its export, because it had been commissioned by the family for the Pucci Chapel in Santissima Annunziata and so, not surprisingly, was regarded as public property, belonging to the chapel for which it had been painted. But Lord Normanby, the British Minister in Florence, was able to negotiate an export licence and the picture arrived in London, together with Filippino Lippi's Rucellai Altarpiece, *Virgin and Child with Saints Jerome and Dominic* (NG 293), in April 1857.

The greatest triumph of 1857 was the acquisition in November 1857 of twenty two pictures from the collection of Francesco Lombardi and Ugo Baldi, which had first been offered for sale in 1838. Eastlake originally suggested that the Gallery should acquire the entire collection, but Mündler was able to negotiate the acquisition of what he described as 'all the justly celebrated and all the most historically valuable pictures' for £7,035. They included Margarito of Arezzo's *The Virgin and Child Enthroned* (NG 564), still the earliest work in the collection and which Eastlake defended in the annual report as showing 'the rude beginnings from which, through nearly two centuries and a half, Italian art slowly advanced to the period of Raphael and his contemporaries'; Duccio's *Virgin and Child with Saints* (NG 565); and, most spectacularly, Uccello's *Battle of San Romano* (NG 583), one of three great battle-pieces painted by Uccello and which came from the Palazzo Medici in Florence, another of which had already been acquired by the Louvre, while the third remains in the Uffizi.

It is clear that, having started with works from the later fifteenth century, Eastlake was extending his view of an appropriate art-historical narrative back into earlier periods of Italian art, with an interest in showing the evolution of Italian painting, as well as in acquiring great works of art in their own right. This followed the precepts of Ruskin, who had been arguing the benefits of viewing pictures in the context of other works of the same period ever since the 1840s, writing in 1857 how 'the character of each picture would be better understood by seeing them together'. Or, as Gustav Waagen wrote in the catalogue of the great Manchester *Art Treasures* exhibition of 1857,

> each work of Art appears as a link in a great chain, which receives an influence from the one preceding it, and imparts an influence to the one following. Each work is thus illustrated and made intelligible, while instruction is combined with enjoyment.

By July 1859, Eastlake was prepared to admit in a letter to Gladstone that the Gallery's requirement for early Italian paintings, particularly of the Florentine and Sienese schools, had been 'in a great measure supplied'. He suggested that it might be advisable instead to try to buy 'reasonably priced works of later periods and other countries'. In general, it is clear that he was at least as interested in works of art as what he described as 'specimens' – using characteristically Victorian scientific language – in which their contribution to the study of history is as important as their quality as works of art. As he wrote, 'the historic value of such specimens as characterising periods in art, outweighs or enhances any considerations respecting their intrinsic qualities'.

Not long afterwards, in 1860, Eastlake was able to acquire forty-six pictures in Paris from the Edmond Beaucousin collection (Beaucousin was a collector who lived in Paris in the Boulevard Montmartre), including an example of Rogier van der Weyden's beautiful, devotional work, *The Magdalen Reading* (NG 654); two remarkable early Flemish portraits now attributed to Robert Campin (NG 653.1 and 653.2); Titian's *Madonna and Child with SS. John the Baptist and Catherine of Alexandria* (NG 635); and, most importantly, Bronzino's sensationally sensual, if perhaps slightly frigid *Allegory of Venus and Cupid* (NG 651), which Beaucousin had kept covered by a veil, which the French packers regarded as 'most improper', and which Mündler when he saw it the year before described as 'voluptuous'. Eastlake himself issued instructions to Wornum as to how the picture was to be described in the catalogue: 'I am quite sure that the word 'sensual' will not do to describe the Bronzino . . . if there is a description which can be quoted and misrepresented, you will have clergymen and others interfering and making out a bad case. Let the picture speak for itself.'

This group reveals the range of Eastlake's tastes and the extent to which it had been formed by his studies for the publication of his *Materials for the History of Oil-Painting* – his ability to admire the quality of works by Bronzino as well as by Duccio and of northern European art as well as Italian.

In 1860, Eastlake was able to turn his attention to the problem of the National Gallery's building and to commission James Pennethorne to add an extension behind the existing building. Following his appointment as Director in 1855, the National Gallery Site Commission had been set up to examine the whole question of a move to another site and of the possible amalgamation of the National Gallery with the art and architecture department of the British Museum. In June 1856, a bill was introduced to parliament suggesting that the National Gallery should move to South Kensington. But the proposal was controversial and viewed as evidence of the malign influence of Prince Albert, who, owing to his involvement in the Great Exhibition, had strong interests in the development of the South Kensington Museum. Although the bill was passed, it was subsequently dropped by Palmerston, an indication that the majority preferred the idea of the National Gallery being situated in the centre of the city, conveniently accessible to as many people as possible, rather than being exiled to the newly developed, middle-class suburb of South Kensington. Instead, Pennethorne was, once again, encouraged to draw up proposals for a picture gallery behind Wilkins's entrance hall, with room for a sculpture gallery in the basement below. Work finally began on Pennethorne's suggestions in 1860.

In a debate in the House of Commons on 18 August 1860, the Liberal MP, Sir Patrick O'Brien, called the National Gallery 'a disgrace to the country . . . to be characterised more fitly as a barrack'. Foreigners who had been to 'Munich, Turin, Dresden, Florence, Paris or Rome, were astonished at the way art in Britain was looked after'. As a result of this debate, parliament voted £15,000 and the Gallery was closed for a period of eight months in order to allow for the alteration of the main entrance and for various other improvements to the heating, lighting and ventilation.

The Gallery reopened on 11 May 1861. There were new staircases to the National Gallery on the left and to the Royal Academy on the right and a grand 75-foot long picture gallery straight ahead, on the site of the current central hall, with a barrel vault and skylights of embossed plate glass. The new gallery was hung with works from the High Renaissance. Limitations of space still required it to be double hung, but it at least allowed the other galleries to be devoted to national schools, thereby fulfilling Eastlake's requirement that the galleries should be laid out more systematically and the Prime Minister's that it should be 'instructive as well as pleasing to the eye of the connoisseur'. The paintings were all photographed and there were experiments with new wall colours, including yellow in the first room hung with early Italian pictures (this was changed to crimson in time for the opening) and green paper in the new north room, which the Keeper Ralph Wornum intensely disliked and which the *Art Journal* described as 'a pale green paper, cold and repugnant to the last degree'.

No sooner had Pennethorne's new gallery opened than William Cowper, the First Commissioner of Works, began to investigate a suggestion that the National Gallery should move to Burlington House on the north side of Piccadilly, leaving the building in Trafalgar Square to the Royal Academy. So, in August 1861, Pennethorne drew up plans for a major new building round a courtyard on the land immediately behind Burlington House.

In December 1863, Lord Palmerston announced in the House of Commons that he thought that the best solution for the long-term future of the National Gallery was for it to be accommodated in 'an unpretentious building in Burlington Gardens between the present house and Savile Row, with no ornament except towards Savile Row'. The commission for its design was given not to Pennethorne, but to Charles Barry junior and his partner, Robert Richardson Banks, as compensation for not winning the competition for the Foreign Office. Early the following year, they talked to Ralph Wornum about the brief for the building and took away copies of the catalogues of the galleries in Dresden and Vienna in order to study their ground plans. It was proposed that there should be a 'great Italian gallery', large enough to house the Mantegnas from Hampton Court. But the proposals ran into difficulties in the House of Commons on the grounds that the position off Piccadilly was too out of the way and that the better of the two sites should not be given to the Royal Academy.

Instead, Cowper decided to buy the workhouse immediately north of the Wilkins building and asked Pennethorne to draw up plans for a northern extension. By now enough time had passed for Pennethorne to appreciate some of the qualities of Wilkins's façade and he proposed keeping it and building behind. He did not want to change the Gallery's character from that of 'a Classic Gallery' to that of 'an Italian Palace'.

By the time of his death on 24 December 1865, not only had Eastlake managed to transform the quality and character of the collection, but he had also begun to resolve the problems of the building in Trafalgar Square, leaving a spacious new gallery, which now no longer exists, and plans for the development of the site behind. During his period of office, the National Gallery remained extremely popular, with 962,128 visitors in 1859, which the Keeper calculated as being equivalent to ten every minute, and evening opening on three evenings a week. He had also embarked on a big manuscript catalogue of the collection, which included entries for each painting under the following headings: 'Painter', 'Subject', 'Number in Gallery', 'Sight Measure', 'Measure including Frame', 'On what Material painted', 'In what Method painted', 'Inscription', 'When repaired', 'Actual State', 'General History'. Space was left at the bottom for subsequent entries noting when 'repairs of any kind were made, or when any appreciable changes in the appearance of the pictures were noticed: together with other circumstances in any way affecting the pictures'. In other words, he was attentive to the documentation of pictures and their treatment.

Eastlake continued to acquire works adventurously right up until his death. For example, in 1860, he acquired Fra Angelico's *Christ glorified in the Court of Heaven* (NG 663), for which he had to pay a special tax of £700 to the papal government to make it possible for it to be exported. In April 1861, he acquired Piero della Francesca's magnificently cool, cerebral painting of *The Baptism of Christ* (NG 665) at a Christie's sale for £241, after it had been bought three years previously by John Charles Robinson from the cathedral authorities in Borgo San Sepolcro in Italy. Eastlake wrote to Layard that 'It is a most undoubted & characteristic specimen, fortunately almost unrestored, & so it will remain – but the great objection to it is its very ruined state. This weighs with me so much that I am at the moment undecided whether to place it in the N. Gallery (where it cannot have a good place) or to take it myself.' In the event, he kept it for himself and it only came to the National Gallery after his death. In July, he bought a number of Quattrocento works, including Filippo Lippi's *Seven Saints* (NG 667) and Crivelli's *The Vision of the Blessed Gabriele* (NG 668), from Alexander Barker, a *marchand amateur*.

Finally, and perhaps most importantly, Eastlake was able to conclude the negotiations for Raphael's *Garvagh Madonna*

(NG 744) not long before his death. Eastlake had an accumulated balance of more than £15,000 in the Gallery's acquisition fund and persuaded Gladstone to seek the consent of Cabinet to the purchase, which was required owing to it costing £9,000.

The Gallery never again quite equalled the range of the acquisitions that it was able to make in the late 1850s, before there was much competition from other museums and galleries abroad which led to a great increase in the price of works of art in the early 1860s, before English owners themselves began to sell, when the laws governing the export of works of art from Italy were still reasonably liberal, and when the Eastlakes were able to travel through Italy buying what they wanted.

# 6. SIR WILLIAM BOXALL
## 1865–74

Following Eastlake's death in Pisa in December 1865, the position of Director was offered to Austen Henry Layard, a former archaeologist in the near east, who had returned to England as an MP and was an under-secretary at the Foreign Office. A passionate collector, born with Filippino Lippi's Rucellai Altarpiece hanging in his bedroom above the bed, Layard held strong views about the decadence of contemporary art and about the appropriate methods of management of museums, particularly of the National Gallery, which he regarded as 'bungling, dilatory, unbusinesslike' by contrast to museums in Berlin, Dresden and Munich. But Layard was not able to accept and was, instead, made a Trustee, able to exert influence over what was collected until his death in Venice in 1894. Queen Victoria wanted John Charles Robinson, the superintendent of art in South Kensington, to be appointed, but he was regarded as too much of a dealer. So, the position was offered instead to William Boxall, the son of a tax official, who had trained at the Royal Academy schools as a mythological painter and was a close friend of the Eastlakes (he was Charles Eastlake's executor). He was a slightly saturnine bachelor, who suffered from depression, admired the paintings of Whistler, and owned a dog called Garibaldi.

Like Eastlake, Boxall travelled abroad every year and, in his first year as Director, acquired Baldovinetti's *Portrait of a Lady in Yellow* (NG 758), then attributed to Piero, and the two Allegories from a series representing the Liberal Arts, which had been painted for the Duke of Urbino and which, when purchased, were attributed to Melozzo da Forlì, although now attributed to Justus of Ghent (NG 755 and 756). Unlike Eastlake, Boxall did not regard the collection of early Italian paintings as remotely adequate and recorded in the 1866 Annual Report that on his journey abroad 'I became convinced that instead of considering our collections of early Italian masters as complete, we ought gladly to avail ourselves of every opportunity of adding to it any really worthy specimens of these earnest and conscientious labourers'.

In practice, it was already becoming much more difficult to acquire works of art in Italy, although this did not prevent Henry Cole, the Director of the South Kensington Museum, from making efforts to buy Giotto's Arena Chapel in Padua in 1868 and ship it back to England. As Boxall wrote to Layard in June 1866:

> The Italian Government has set its seal and has inventoried every work of art in every church or fraternity worth having! Every significant work of art must be first offered to the Italian Government. Morelli says that the Government has collected together all the fine things from all the churches . . . and made its selection for a great national gallery in Florence *(a wild vision)* we shall be the first to whom a specimen of any particular school we may require shall be offered.

The following year, he wrote in similar terms to Layard to say that 'The government has put its seal upon every picture belonging not only to the Church but to the confraternities so that I can do nothing. I cannot blame the Italians for their decision to keep their finest works at home.' Boxall was also concerned that prices had reached 'such a pitch' that 'only millionaires or madmen could buy' works of art.

These difficulties did not prevent Boxall from acquiring both Crivelli's fine Demidoff Altarpiece (NG 788.1) for

£3,360 and Michelangelo's *Entombment* (NG 790) in 1868. In buying the Michelangelo, he was apparently influenced by the advice of Giovanni Morelli, the great advocate of the principles of scientific connoisseurship, who had visited England in July 1868 and been shown the Michelangelo by Layard. As Layard wrote to Sir William Gregory:

> The day before I left England Boxall concluded the bargain with Macpherson for the Michelangelo. We had to pay £2000 for it – but he could not have obtained it for less. I am glad that he has purchased it, as it is really a great picture, altho' a fragment, and will be a very important addition to our gallery. Boxall was a great deal influenced by the opinion of my friend Morelli, the deputy for Bergamo, whom I take to be the best judge of pictures of the Italian schools in the world.

In the early part of Boxall's period of office, there had been much discussion about plans and proposals for a new building for the National Gallery and, in June 1866, the Keeper, Ralph Wornum, drew up a list of possible requirements, including 'Retiring rooms for ladies', a 'Frame and framing room', an Easel room for storing students' easels, stools, and high chairs, and a 'Police Kitchen, with lockers for the men'. In the event, the many architects who submitted proposals for the public competition in 1867 were simply given the option of either 'retaining the existing building' (without the Royal Academy in the eastern part), or of 'reconstructing or remodelling it'. Most chose the latter, ignoring Boxall's belief that 'the Building should be a Picture Gallery – not a cathedral nor a Theatre'. The only requirement was that there should be as much hanging space as possible 'consistent with grand architectural effects', and in most of the competition entries, grand architectural effects were superabundantly evident, with a profusion of domes and over-ostentatious interiors and including proposals for a gothic gallery by G.E. Street.

In the end, the competition was won by Edward Middleton Barry, the architect of the Royal Opera House, third son of Sir Charles Barry, with a proposal for a grand, new, Italianate building, and throughout the remainder of Boxall's period of office, there was discussion about the appropriate form of the new building, including a suggestion in 1868, after Layard had been appointed First Commissioner, that it should be moved to a new site on the embankment and that the design should include space for the Raphael Cartoons, the British Museum's collection of prints and drawings, and a gallery of contemporary European art.

Meanwhile, Boxall was continuing to add to the collection. In 1869, he bought Pieter de Hooch's *Woman and her Maid in a Courtyard* (NG 794) from the sale of Baron Delessert's collection and, in 1871, he was able to negotiate the acquisition of Sir Robert Peel's entire collection of paintings *en bloc* for £75,000, on condition that the regular purchase grant of £10,000 was temporarily suspended. The sixty-nine Flemish and Dutch pictures in the Peel collection, which had been acquired through the agency of dealers mainly during the 1820s and hung in his house in Whitehall Gardens, included Rubens's *Chapeau de Paille* (NG 852), which was used as the model for a portrait by Sir Thomas Lawrence of Peel's wife, and Van Dyck's *Triumph of Silenus* (NG 853); two more great works by de Hooch (NG 834 and 835); four pictures by Hobbema, including *The Avenue, Middelharnis* (NG 830) and *The Ruins of Brederode Castle* (NG 831); three landscapes by Cuyp (NG 822, 823 and 824); and ter Borch's *Young Woman playing a Theorbo to Two Men* (NG 864). It also contained pictures by lesser Dutch masters, including seven by Willem van der Velde the Younger (NG 870–6) and five by Wouwermans (NG 878–82). At a stroke the National

Gallery's holdings of Dutch paintings were transformed, providing a better balance in the collection to the overwhelming strength of its holdings of early Italian art.

Towards the end of his life, Boxall grew lazy and was described by Layard as 'hopelessly idle in his old age'. But he was to make one last great purchase in 1873 when the Treasury made a special grant to enable the Gallery to acquire Mantegna's *Introduction of the Cult of Cybele at Rome* (NG 902).

# 7. SIR FREDERIC BURTON
## 1874–94

In February 1874, Boxall was succeeded by Sir Frederic Burton, an Irish watercolour painter with a strong interest in Irish antiquities, who, in 1842, visited Germany to sketch Bavarian peasants and was employed by King Maximilian II of Bavaria to make copies of pictures in the royal collection. Thomas Carlyle met him in Dublin in 1849 and described him as 'thin, aquiline, with long thin locks scattered about with a look of real painter talent, but proud, vain; not a pleasant man of genius'. In 1851, he settled in Germany where he acquired an exceptional knowledge of the German galleries and his painting was influenced by the Nazarenes, before moving back to London in 1858, where, not surprisingly, he made friends with Boxall and other artists and collectors in the circle of Dante Gabriel Rossetti.

Burton quickly acquired a special grant to buy works at the sale in June 1874 of Alexander Barker's collection. Although it was particularly strong in Venetian paintings, Burton bought works from central Italy – Piero della Francesca's earthy depiction of *The Nativity* (NG 908), even then not in good condition, Botticelli's incredibly pagan *Venus and Mars* (NG 915) and two frescoes from the Petrucci palace at Siena, Signorelli's *Triumph of Chastity* (NG 910) and Pintoricchio's *Scenes from the Odyssey* (NG 911). Disraeli took a personal interest in the Barker sale, spent a morning with Burton discussing it, and wrote to the Countess of Bradford on 2 June 1874: 'If the Barker pictures are so rare and wondrous as I hear, it shall go hard if the nation does not possess them', revealing the political appetite to continue to add adventurously to the National Gallery's collection.

In 1876, the collection was enriched by a big bequest from Wynne Ellis, a London haberdasher who had made a fortune out of silk. On 10 April 1876 the Board 'selected ninety-four works, by 56 masters, viz: Fourteen pictures, by eleven Flemish masters; Three pictures, by two French masters, and one described as Spanish'. The Bequest included two beautiful small works from the fifteenth century – Antonio Pollaiuolo's tiny *Apollo and Daphne* (NG 928) and the Dirk Bouts *Portrait of a Man* (NG 943). But the collection was strongest, like Peel's, in Dutch pictures, including two landscapes by Cuyp, *The Large Dort* (NG 961) and *The Small Dort* (NG 962), four river scenes by van de Cappelle (NG 964–7), a landscape by Hobbema (NG 995) and three by Jacob van Ruisdael (NG 986, 988 and 990), including the fine *Extensive Landscape with a Ruined Castle and a Village Church* (NG 990). Ellis had also owned three important Canalettos (NG 937, 938 and 942), including *The Feast Day of St Roch* (NG 937).

The year 1876 also saw the opening of E.M. Barry's new galleries behind the Wilkins Building. The result was far less ostentatious than the original proposals with which he had won the 1867 competition, but the galleries were still fairly ornate, with a marble floor in the cross-axis and extremely opulent ceiling decoration in the octagon. Their general mood is perhaps best expressed by the inscription which Barry proposed for the central room and which was a quotation from Sir Joshua Reynolds: 'The works of those who stood the test of ages have a claim to that respect and veneration to which no modern can pretend'. A high rail protected the pictures, the walls had dark maroon embossed wallpaper, and there was a heavy black marble dado below the pictures. In the basement, where there are now long corridors and small offices, the rooms were expected to accommodate students.

In terms of the arrangement of the collection, the British School now occupied the entire west wing to the left of the main staircase, as well as two galleries of the east, which were followed by a French gallery, and (in the easternmost room) the Italian, French and Dutch works of the Wynne Ellis Bequest. Meanwhile, the new Barry rooms were used to display the early Italian paintings and, in the octagon, a mixture of works from the Peel collection. *The Builder* lamented the fact that the opportunity had not been taken to demolish Wilkins's 'grim and dreary-looking' building.

Looking back on the arguments about the best location for the National Gallery, the opening of the Barry Rooms in 1876 appears as the moment when all the public discussion about where the National Gallery should be, what it should include, and whether or not the original Wilkins building should be demolished, finally came to an end. It now owned both halves of the Wilkins Building. The Royal Academy had relocated to a new building, including exhibition galleries and an art school, constructed at the back of Burlington House on Piccadilly. And the site on Trafalgar Square had plenty of space to the north for future development.

After buying Leonardo's gloriously mysterious *The Virgin of the Rocks* (NG 1093) for £9,000 in 1880, the Gallery switched its attention from buying overseas and relying on bequests from British collectors like Wynne Ellis to trying, often in vain, to save works of art from being exported abroad either to museums in Germany or private collections in the United States of America. Wilhelm Bode, the curator and later Director of what was to become the Kaiser Friedrich Museum in Berlin, was active in the London sale room and the great plutocrats on the other side of the Atlantic were beginning to take an interest in the acquisition of art. The

1880s saw the beginnings of the great sales of the grand, aristocratic collections in English country houses, prompted by an agricultural depression, declining rents, and the introduction of death duties. Land was worth less and works of art more. So, landowners, who have always been canny about how best to exploit their assets, chose to sell. As a result, the National Gallery changed from being an institution which was able to acquire works of art aggressively from collections abroad to one which was increasingly preoccupied with buying works of art from British private collections as and when they were sold in the London auction rooms.

The first great aristocratic sale was of the collection of the twelfth Duke of Hamilton in 1882, which included many of the pictures which had been acquired by William Beckford earlier in the century and, according to *The Times* 'attracted dealers and amateurs from all Europe and America'. A special exchequer grant of £15,600 made it possible for the Gallery to acquire two more large Renaissance altarpieces, Botticini's *Assumption of the Virgin* (NG 1126), then attributed to Botticelli, and Signorelli's *Circumcision* (NG 1128), as well as a number of smaller Italian pictures, including Cima's *S. Jerome in a Landscape* (NG 1120). But the greatest of the pictures acquired at this sale was the full-length portrait by Velázquez of *Philip IV of Spain in Brown and Silver* (NG 1129), bought for £6,300 and an indication of an increasing interest during the 1880s in Spanish art, inspired by the writings of Richard Ford.

It was at the Hamilton Palace sale that use was first made of the Clarke Bequest – £24,000 bequeathed by Mr Francis Clarke in 1856 and put at the Gallery's disposal after the death of his son in 1879. From this fund Pontormo's *Joseph in Egypt* (NG 1131) and Tintoretto's *Christ washing his Disciple's Feet* (NG 1130) were bought; and, in 1883, two small predella panels from Duccio's *Maestà* were acquired from Charles Fairfax Murray, a painter, copyist and dealer who lived in Florence – *The Annunciation* (NG 1139) and *Jesus opens the Eyes of a Man born Blind* (NG 1140).

The next great sale was of pictures from the eighth Duke of Marlborough's collection at Blenheim Palace. In spring 1884, the Duke, who had succeeded in 1883 and immediately sold Blenheim's great library, contacted the Trustees and suggested that they might like to select a group of paintings from Blenheim. They initially chose Raphael's *Ansidei Madonna*, Van Dyck's *Equestrian Portrait of Charles I*, *A Seaport in Spain* by Weenix, Mytens's portrait of the second Duke of Hamilton, Sebastiano's *Portrait of a Lady* and seven works by Rubens, including two portraits of Helena Fourment. The Duke asked for £400,000 for these works, a price that was exponentially more than the Gallery had ever paid for any previous group of acquisitions. Even when the list was reduced to only five, the price was still £165,000.

For the first time, it was clear that there was no way in which the National Gallery was going to be able to acquire works at this price. Frederic Leighton, the President of the Royal Academy, organised an appeal to the Prime Minister in which he wrote how 'The rumour that a large number of pictures are about to be offered for sale, pictures amongst which are counted works unique in their excellence and beauty, has strongly moved the artistic community in this country'. He hoped that 'we be spared the humiliation of seeing them pass into those foreign hands, which are, as we too well know, eager to receive them'.

A memorandum from Burton and his Trustees to Gladstone described how 'The incorporation of these works in the English National Collection would at once raise it to a rank second to none and superior to most of the great Continental Galleries'. In a subsequent personal letter, Burton described the classic dilemma of the National Gallery that 'the value of any great production of genius in money is a thing not easily determined. It resolves itself simply into a question of what the vendors will take and the purchaser give for an article combining the highest qualities with extreme rarity'.

The Trustees were allowed to offer £100,000 for the three most desirable pictures. The Duke of Westminster led a delegation to see the Chancellor of the Exchequer, who described how 'he could never forget that this Country had a great deal of lost ground to make up in consequence of the dispersion of the splendid collection of works of art made by Charles I, now for the most part at the Louvre, or the Hermitage or at Madrid'. Frederic Harrison 'spoke warmly of the interest shown by the working classes . . . and expressed his opinion that they were invariably in favour of the purchase of great works of art, even at very high prices, when recommended by those who were conversant with such matters'. And the Earl of Wemyss quoted a remark of Benjamin Jowett, the Master of Balliol College, Oxford that 'the Country does not feel the expenditure of money on fine works of art, but always feels regret when an opportunity is missed of acquiring them'. A resolution was signed by sixty-four Members of the House of Commons and published a few days later, which reassured the Government 'that to the best of our belief our Constituents and the whole Nation will approve and applaud an expenditure, even though so large . . .'

But, in spite of all this campaigning, making the public case for the importance of the National Gallery and its collection, the government stood firm. The Gallery was able to acquire only Raphael's *Ansidei Madonna* (NG 1171) and Van Dyck's great *Equestrian Portrait of Charles I* (NG 1172) for £70,000 in August 1889.

While these negotiations were taking place, the Gallery opened the new main staircase which still survives, opening out from Wilkins's portico, and a central gallery, both of which were designed by the government's architect, Sir John

Taylor, and which involved the demolition of Pennethorne's gallery.

The decoration of the staircase hall, which has recently been restored after being whitewashed in the 1930s, was redolent of the last period of great confidence in the National Gallery's history. It was the work of the Craces, a firm of decorators then at the apex of its success under John Dibblee Crace and which had been responsible for the interiors at Knighthayes in Devon, the Pompeian Room at Ickworth, and the wonderful series of ornate state rooms at Longleat which were specially installed to show the collection of the fourth Marquess of Bath. As *The Builder* commented in its report of the National Gallery's new interiors, when they opened in September 1887: 'The staircase depends for its effect more upon the material employed, and the decoration executed by Messrs Crace and Son, than upon any stroke of architectural genius', and the *Journal of Decorative Art* felt that 'One thing is certain and that is, the pictures look finer in the newly decorated rooms than in the older parts of the building'.

If the 1880s represented a period of confidence, it was not to last. The year 1889 was, in many ways, a turning point for the Gallery. It was the first year when its purchase grant was reduced, from £10,000 to £5,000, just at the moment when prices were beginning to escalate, making great paintings increasingly unaffordable. It was the year when the Prime Minister, Lord Salisbury, announced at the Royal Academy's annual dinner that the land immediately north of the National Gallery was going to be allocated to the National Portrait Gallery, thereby depriving it of space to expand in the future. And, in March 1890, Henry Tate, the Liverpool sugar manufacturer, announced the gift to the nation of his collection of British art, with the proviso that they were displayed in a room bearing his name.

Tate's gift compelled the National Gallery to acknowledge that the imbalance between the British collection and works of other schools was now unmanageable. It declined the gift and, instead, after long negotiations, Tate agreed to pay for a new, so-called 'National Gallery of British Art' on the site of the old penitentiary at Millbank down river beyond the Palace of Westminster.

Given the extreme inadequacy of government funding, it is perhaps not surprising that 1890 was also the year that the National Gallery first turned to private individuals to help fund acquisitions. The Earl of Radnor, caught by the high costs of running Longford Castle, the family's Elizabethan castle outside Salisbury, and by the necessity of paying inheritance tax, had come to the conclusion that he needed to sell some of the greatest works from his collection, including Holbein's group portrait of *The Ambassadors* (NG 1314), which had been bought by the second Earl of Radnor in 1811, and *Portrait of a Gentleman* (NG 1316), previously attributed to Titian, but recognised by Eastlake as by Moroni, for £55,000. Three private individuals, Lord Rothschild, Sir Edward Guinness and Charles Cotes, each gave £10,000 on condition that the balance of £25,000 was paid by the Treasury in a special exchequer grant.

By the 1890s, the audience for the National Gallery also seems to have changed. In the middle part of the century, there is a great deal of anecdotal and other evidence, including surveys as to who visited amongst local employers, that it was visited by the so-called 'working man'. By the end of the century, the expansion of the city into the more distant suburbs meant that there was much less fluidity in the geography of London and more segregation of neighbourhoods. The writings of Walter Pater had replaced those of John Ruskin as the bible for the art-loving, middle classes. Pater's emphasis on the solitary and mystic communion with art as opposed to the moral uplift of its subject matter and his belief that the experience of art was akin to religion made the mood of the National Gallery more etiolated, less open to the working classes, while the middle classes concentrated their efforts on social improvement in the new galleries like the Whitechapel Art Gallery and the South London Art Gallery in Camberwell. An examination of the visitors depicted in Giuseppe Gabrielli's *Room 32 in the National Gallery* (the northernmost of the group of new galleries designed by E.M. Barry), which was painted in 1886, suggests that they were the *bourgeoisie*, the men nearly all wearing top hats, the women in crinolines, and even the warders dressed up in immaculate uniform, with elegant red piping to their long coats. In 1886 the Trustees considered the possibility of once more introducing evening opening, but this time rejected it. Charles Holmes, who was his successor-but-two, remembered Sir Frederic Burton, who only visited the National Gallery for an hour a day in the afternoon, 'hanging pictures in a smart gray frock-coat and lilac gloves'. He was almost certainly not thinking of how the pictures would benefit the working-classes.

# 8. SIR EDWARD POYNTER
## 1894–1904

Following the retirement of Sir Frederic Burton in March 1894, there was a certain amount of public discussion as to who should succeed him. D.S. MacColl, a high-minded and sometimes acerbic Scottish critic on the *Saturday Review*, argued in favour of the appointment of Sidney Colvin, the Keeper of Prints at the British Museum, on the grounds that the post now required a scholar, not a painter:

> The study of the older schools of painting has become in recent times a branch of archaeology pursued like other branches of archaeology by specialists, who have the time and the patience to acquire a vast deal of exact knowledge. This exact knowledge, founded on a study of the public and private collections of Europe, on the comparison of drawings with pictures, coupled with the evidence of documents, and dealing with the derivation, the likeness, the difference of masters and schools, the number of authentic pictures, the number and kind of copies and forgeries in existence has been growing yearly.

The advice was ignored. Instead, the person appointed, Sir Edward Poynter, was a *grand seigneur* of the late Victorian art world, the great-grandson of the sculptor Thomas Banks, son of the architect, Ambrose Poynter, and so born into the purple of the Victorian art aristocracy. Trained under Thomas Shotter Boys and at the Royal Academy Schools, he had been an extremely diligent and ambitious student in Paris, the model for Lorrimer in George du Maurier's *Trilby*, who was described as 'a painstaking young enthusiast, of precocious culture, who read improving books, and did not share the amusement of the quartier latin, but spent his evenings at home with Handel, Michael Angelo and Dante, on the respectable side of the river'.

On his return from Paris, Poynter made his reputation with grand, mythological paintings of ancient Rome, Pompeii and Egypt and was also involved in the revival of mosaic, working on the walls of the lecture theatre at the South Kensington Museum and the grill room below. In 1871, he became the first Slade Professor of Fine Art at University College, London and, four years later, he was appointed Director of Art at the National Art Training School in South Kensington. As a student in Paris, he had been passionate about Old Master paintings and his appointment was strongly recommended by his brother-in-law, Edward Burne-Jones, who rejoiced that 'he's a fine fellow to consent to put by part of his own work for the public good – public good – no d—n the public – private good – the good of the half dozen who really care'. Tall, bearded and rather forbidding, he was the epitome of what a Director should be.

But, however well qualified as Director, the Treasury took the opportunity of Poynter's appointment to curb his powers in the so-called Rosebery Minute, dated 26 April 1894, which transferred the authority for acquisition away from the Director back to the Board of Trustees. It was claimed that 'the Trustees, while apparently occupying a position of authority and responsibility are debarred from the exercise of any real power, and this appears to Lord Rosebery to constitute an anomaly which should if possible be removed'. It was now stated that

a Board of competent persons – not necessarily
experts, but selected with a due regard to their special

qualifications for the work, and applied with the best
expert assistance – possesses an advantage which cannot
be so effectively obtained under a system which places
the whole responsibility for a decision on the shoulders
of one individual.

What lay behind the Rosebery Minute was partly a conflict of authority (Burton was regarded as having been too
independent-minded) and partly a long-standing tension
between the Trustees, who wanted only to acquire obvious
masterpieces, and the Directors and their staff, including
both Burton and Poynter, who tended to have more catholic
and art-historical tastes and were interested in the acquisition of works which may have seemed at the time to be
of more specialist interest. When the Chancellor of the
Exchequer, William Harcourt, criticised the acquisition of
pictures which he regarded as by unimportant Dutch masters (so-called 'little curios'), Poynter replied that 'de Hooghe
is to me such an exceptionally charming artist that I should
always like to add a good one to the Gallery when there is a
chance of getting one'.

When Poynter returned from a trip on the continent just
after his appointment and announced that he had bought
three canvasses from the Scarpa collection at Milan, including Gaudenzio Ferrari's beautiful *Christ Rising from the
Tomb* (NG 1465) and Lelio Orsi's *The Walk to Emmaus* (NG
1466) they were denounced by two Trustees, the Marquess of
Lansdowne and Alfred de Rothschild, as the purchases of a
fool. Rothschild, who was a prominent aesthete and had a private circus at Halton, his country house in Buckinghamshire,
claimed responsibility for the Rosebery minute and believed
passionately that the National Gallery should only acquire
masterpieces. When Bronzino's *Portrait of a Lady* came up
for sale in 1896, offered at £1,400, Rothschild described the

picture as 'ugly' and in 1897 he thought Holbein's *Christina of Denmark* (NG 2475) 'unworthy' of the collection.

The 1890s were altogether a bad decade for the National Gallery. In 1894, the Trustees were offered one of Titian's greatest mythological paintings, the *Rape of Europa*, for sale by the sixth Earl of Darnley for a mere £15,000. They could not afford it. It was bought, instead, by Isabella Stewart Gardner two years later, acting on the advice of the young Bernard Berenson. The sale of Rembrandt's *Renier Ansloo* from the Ashburnham Collection to Berlin in 1894 caused widespread protests in the press (although the following year the Gallery was able to acquire Pisanello's *The Vision of St Eustace* (NG 1436) from the same collection). In 1898, Mrs Gardner acquired Rubens's great portrait of Thomas Howard, Earl of Arundel from the Earl of Warwick, without it being offered to the National Gallery, and, in the following year, she bought Fra Angelico's *Dormition* and *Assumption of the Virgin* from Lord Methuen at Corsham. In 1901, the Museum of Fine Arts in Boston acquired Velázquez's portrait of *Prince Balthasar Carlos, aged two, with his Dwarf* from the ninth Earl of Carlisle, who seems to have sold paintings from the collection at Castle Howard without necessarily offering them to the National Gallery first, in spite of the fact that he was a long-serving and devoted Trustee.

The balance of advantage in major acquisitions had tilted away from the National Gallery first towards foreign museums, especially the Berlin Museum under Wilhelm Bode, and then to private collections in America, including those of Pierpont Morgan, Henry Clay Frick, and Isabella Stewart Gardner. John Charles Robinson, the great connoisseur and art referee at the South Kensington Museum, complained that the Germans were 'robbing us of the very springs and bases of connoisseurship, the noble art treasures which our fathers and grandfathers endowed us with, whilst we waste our money on second-rate curiosities only, or worthless trash'.

As a result of the loss of pictures overseas, D.S. MacColl suggested in 1900 that there ought to be a Friends of the National Gallery on the model of the *Société des Amis du Louvre* and the *Kaiser Friedrich Museums Verein*, which could lobby on its behalf for funding. This led to the establishment of the National Art-Collections Fund on 7 July 1903 at the house of Christiana Herringham, an expert on egg tempera painting and translator of Cennino Cennini's treatise *Il libro dell'arte*. Sir Robert Witt described the reason for its foundation twenty-five years later:

> The art treasures of this country were rapidly passing
> abroad, prices were rising against the Museums and
> Galleries, the purchase grants were stationary or
> diminishing, the attitude of the authorities was one
> of helplessness or despair. Public opinion was uneasy,
> indeed, but unorganized and ineffective, and there was
> no nucleus round which it could rally to the rescue of all
> that was being steadily dissipated.

The British decided to fight back against 'the multi-millionaires of the New World'.

When Poynter bought a Jordaens in 1902 without the Trustees' prior approval, Lansdowne proposed restricting his power of purchase still further. In particular, he recommended that no painting should be purchased unless agreed to by a minimum of four Trustees (not including the Director) and that all paintings under consideration must be made available for inspection by all Trustees at least three days before such a meeting. These became known as the 'Lansdowne Resolutions'. Only Lord Carlisle objected, describing how 'The National Gallery has been built up under the constitution of 1855, by a series of able and devoted Directors. I have serious doubts as to whether the initiative and guidance of a competent Director can be satisfactorily replaced by the joint action of a Board, however able or distinguished the members of that Board may be individually.'

By 1904, Poynter was fed up with the interference of his autocratic Trustees, their indecision and lack of moral support. Aged sixty-eight, he decided not to seek renewal of his appointment.

## 9. SIR CHARLES HOLROYD
### 1906–17

The Treasury prevaricated over whether or not to appoint Roger Fry, the brilliant painter, critic and art historian, as the relevant Treasury official was not convinced that Fry was suitably qualified, in spite of the range of his publications, although he was very impressed by the fact that Fry's father was a high court judge. So, Fry went to New York instead to work as an adviser to Pierpont Morgan at the Metropolitan Museum, leaving the question open as one of the more intriguing counter-factuals of the National Gallery's history as to what would have happened had Fry been appointed, at a time when he was still much more of an authority on Old Master paintings than on contemporary art and when he had all the energy of a young member of the Bloomsbury set.

As when Poynter had been appointed, there was much public discussion about what were the proper characteristics of a Director. For example, the *Burlington Magazine* argued that 'Critical knowledge is . . . far more essential than administrative capacity' and a letter to *The Times* asked if the new Director was 'to be, as in the past, the mere servant of the Trustees or is he to be given the powers which are essential to efficient administration? On the former hypothesis it really matters little who the Director may be, for the real control will be exercised by the Trustees.' The post was eventually offered to Charles Holroyd, an arts-and-crafts etcher, who had been a star pupil of Alphonse Legros at the Slade School and was appointed the first Keeper of the Tate Gallery on its foundation in 1897. He had a tough time as Director. Not long after he was appointed, Alfred de Rothschild graphically described how 'if he were one's butler and brought up a corked bottle of wine one would spit it out', suggestive of his general contempt for Holroyd's expertise.

During the interregnum, Velázquez's *Rokeby Venus* (NG 2057) had come onto the market. According to Major H.E. Morritt, who sold the picture, it was first offered to the Trustees of the National Gallery for £25,000, although there is no evidence of this. It was then offered for sale through Agnew's for £40,000.

The National Art-Collections Fund immediately launched a public appeal with a letter to the Editor of *The Times* dated 9 November 1905:

> Sir, Is it too late to raise a protest against the continued
> apathy of our National Gallery authorities, who, now
> for decade after decade, watch with folded hands
> the steady drain of the finest works of art from this
> country? The famous 'Rokeby' Velasquez, unique in
> subject and supreme in quality, the possession of which
> was one of the glories of England, is now exhibited
> for sale at Messrs. Agnew's. It is useless to lament the
> insensibility and lack of enterprise of the Trustees of the
> National Gallery in allowing such a picture, if for sale
> at all, to come on the public market, without an effort
> to secure it before publicity had raised its price to the
> level it must by now have reached. Incompetence in high
> places has to be paid for by the public, whether it be the
> Army or the National Gallery that is in question. The
> present case is one of such urgency and importance that
> the needful payment should be made – the lesson of it
> may afterwards be taken to heart. That lesson, written
> large for all to read in the splendid Berlin Museum, is
> that expert management and expert freedom, coupled
> with responsibility, are alone efficient, and that our

haphazard boards of amateur Trustees are inept by
comparison.

Most of the press supported the appeal, an article appearing in the *Morning Post* stating that 'No country in Europe
has a collection of paintings equal in variety and quality to
that in our National Gallery. The name we have thus acquired
must be upheld . . . If this project fails it will, to say the least,
throw discredit on us as a nation aspiring to the patronage
of high art.'

By early December, the Fund had raised £15,000 towards
the £40,000 required, including a gift of £10,000 from an
anonymous donor who described himself as 'An Englishman'.
The Treasury refused to help and by the end of December 1905
it looked as if the picture might be lost. But then, Edward VII
apparently intervened. According to a letter pasted to the min-
utes book of the fund's Executive Committee on 24 January
1906, he came to see the picture and pledged £8,000, including a loan of a further £5,000, which effectively secured the
painting. The purchase was announced on 24 January 1906.

In 1906, the National Gallery was also offered an exceptionally important group of Impressionist paintings, including
Manet's *Portrait d'Eva Gonzalès* (NG 3259) and Renoir's
*Les parapluies* (NG 3268), on loan from an Irish dealer and
collector, Hugh Lane, who had a good eye and wide-ranging
taste. Charles Holroyd, new in post, accepted with enthu-
siasm, but was immediately rebuked by his Trustees who
thought that Lane was using the Gallery simply as a show-
room. Lord Redesdale, a recently appointed Trustee, later
described the pictures in evidence to the Curzon Committee
as 'crazy extravagances of modern French decadents' and
Alfred de Rothschild thought the works of Manet 'unnecessary rubbish'. It was a disaster from which the National
Gallery has never fully recovered that the small-mindedness

and snobbery of these two Trustees was able to over-rule the more adventurous tastes of Holroyd.

In the same year, the Gallery was informed that it was to be bequeathed a collection of mostly Italian paintings acquired by Ludwig Mond, who had settled in England in the 1860s and had become one of the great chemical entrepreneurs of the late nineteenth century, creating the company, Brunner Mond, which during the 1920s was to become ICI. On 11 February 1906, Lewis Harcourt, the son of Gladstone's home secretary, a man-about-town and Liberal MP (he was nick-named 'Loulou'), wrote to Sir Charles Holroyd:

> I am not sure whether you are aware (but in any case
> it is as well that I should put it on record) that my
> negotiations with Dr Ludwig Mond have now been
> brought to a satisfactory conclusion. His collection
> of Italian pictures are left by will to the National
> Gallery (I think to his wife for life) and his executors
> are empowered if desirable to build a room or rooms
> attached to the National Gallery for the reception of his
> collection but I understand that the pictures are left with
> as little limitation as possible upon their subsequent
> treatment and disposal in order that the trustees of the
> National Gallery should not be hampered in the matter.
> I am extremely glad to be in any way instrumental in
> securing what I cannot doubt will be a most valuable
> addition to our National Collection.

The paintings did not come to the Gallery till 1924, following the death of Mond's widow, Frida, but it was presumably gratifying to know that a substantial collection, which had been assembled with advice from the German art historian, Jean Paul Richter, and the specific intention that every work should be museum-worthy, was going to come to the

Gallery in due course. It was a highly intelligent collection and included three Bellinis (NG 3911, 3912 and 3913), Fra Bartolommeo's *The Virgin adoring the Child with St Jospeph* (NG 3914), and the so-called Mond *Crucifixion* (NG 3943), which he had acquired at the Dudley sale in 1892.

Another generous bequest was announced in 1909 when the will of George Salting, an eccentric bachelor collector, who was the son of a Danish businessman, was born in Australia and educated at university in Sydney, revealed that he had left his extraordinarily rich and wide-ranging 'Art Collections' to 'the Nation' – that is, to the South Kensington Museum, the British Museum and the National Gallery. The Trustees of the National Gallery were able to select whatever they wanted from his collection and to acquire 164 paintings, including Memling's *A Young Man at Prayer* (NG 2594), Robert Campin's *Virgin and Child before a Fire Screen* (NG 2609), and Vermeer's *A Young Woman Seated at a Virginal* (NG 2568).

In 1909, there was a further *cause célèbre* when the Duke of Norfolk offered Holbein's full-length portrait of *Christina of Denmark* (NG 2475) for sale, prompted, so the Duke claimed, by Lloyd George's so-called 'People's Budget'. The Trustees were given only nine days' notice. They refused. The picture was immediately sold by Colnaghi's to Henry Clay Frick. Once again, there was a public outcry. An article in the *Morning Chronicle* described how

> The Duke of Norfolk belongs to a family which has given many great names to English history. He above all therefore, should understand that the ordinary laws of private property do not apply to his picture by Holbein which has been a national asset. An ordinary millionaire who has made money by gambling on a large scale may be excused if he puts one of the world's

masterpieces into the public market, using the ordinary tricks of the trade to secure a fancy price. But that the premier Duke of England should so far forget his family pride as to expect the highest possible price from his country under the threat of selling his picture to some American or Jewish millionaire abroad is almost incredible and certainly shameful.

The National Art-Collections Fund launched an appeal and, when it appeared that the full amount could not be raised even in spite of the Prime Minister pledging £10,000 at the Royal Academy's annual dinner, an English lady wrote from a spa in Germany that she was willing to provide the necessary funds. Years later, Sir Isidore Spielmann, an engineer who had been prominently involved in international exhibitions, described how they broke the news:

> 'Holroyd, the picture is saved', I said. 'Cheer up my dear fellow; the picture is ours', said my colleague. He looked at us from one to another as if dazed, and then followed the most pathetic incident in the whole of these proceeedings. He buried his face in his hands and burst into tears.

The constant sale of major works of art overseas provoked a great deal of discussion in the newspapers, including an article by Robbie Ross, the friend of Oscar Wilde, in the *Morning Post* which listed the seventy-five important works which had recently been sold abroad and was to inspire a novel by Henry James, *The Outcry*, written to deal with the question as to how far the fortunate owners of precious works of art 'hold them in trust, as it were, for the nation, and may themselves, as lax guardians, be held to account by public opinion'. Charles Holroyd came up with the idea of preparing a national register of pictures of importance, in the expectation that the National Gallery would have the right to buy them, if they were sold. The proposal was published under the title *Memorandum Regarding the Registration of Pictures*. It was not well received, regarded in the press as too authoritarian and too socialist, comparable in spirit to the registration of land undertaken by the Commissioners of the Inland Revenue in 1910.

In 1911, Lord Lansdowne, himself a Trustee and author of the so-called Lansdowne Resolutions, chose to sell Rembrandt's *The Mill* to Joseph Widener in the United States, after it had been exhibited for a mere three weeks in the National Gallery and the Treasury had refused to provide a special purchase grant. Both the *Burlington Magazine* and the *Guardian* wrote articles contrasting the intelligent and far-sighted acquisitions of the German museums, as compared to the incompetence of the National Gallery. As Roger Fry wrote in the *Burlington Magazine*: 'The time has come when it is no longer possible to conceal the deep indignation of those who have the interests of our National Collections at heart . . . it is now our duty to state plainly that the trustees of the National Gallery have, as a body, conspicuously failed in the trust which has been placed upon them.'

In contrast to the majority of Trustees, who behaved pretty badly when it came to the sale of works they themselves owned, defending their right to sell at the highest price, if necessary overseas, while ignoring any sense of moral responsibility to offer the works to the National Gallery first, Rosalind, the public-spirited and strongly socialist widow of George Howard, ninth Earl of Carlisle, acting in accordance with his wishes, offered Jan Gossaert's *Adoration of the Kings* (NG 2790) – the so-called Castle Howard Mabuse – for a reduced price rather than selling it on the open market. She subsequently allowed the Trustees to select twelve other works from the Castle Howard collection, including Annibale Carracci's *Three Maries* (NG 2923), described in 1815 as 'very famous and most justly so', and Rubens's *Portrait of Thomas Howard, Earl of Arundel* (NG 2968).

Just before the First World War, the Trustees of the National Gallery at long last began to address the insistent problems surrounding the lack of available funding. Lord Curzon, the former Viceroy of India, was appointed a Trustee in 1911 and immediately established a committee 'to Enquire into the Retention of Important Pictures in this Country and Other Matters Connected with the National Collections': the language used indicates a new attitude to national interest as opposed to the previous belief in the *laissez-faire* rights of owners. The committee issued a report in 1914 arguing for an increase in the parliamentary grant from £5,000 to £25,000 and for much more frequent special grants to allow major purchases. But, according to Charles Holmes, who was to succeed Holroyd as Director, the report was a fudge. He wrote:

> The Committee certainly collected a mass of facts and opinions bearing on administrative questions, and its Report, issued in 1915 in the form of an official document, was sensible enough upon such simple matters as the Chantrey Bequest, and the best way of managing the Tate Gallery. But on harder and more vital problems – the limitation of the national aims to a few irreplaceable masterpieces; the means to secure these few masterpieces against foreign purchasers, whether by a capital fund or otherwise, and the all-important business of the Director's authority – the issue was discreetly evaded.

Besides, the timing was bad. By the time the Report was published, the country was at war. Officials in the Treasury argued that an increase in the grant would simply lead to inflation in the cost of works of art. The report was, like so many Treasury reports, discreetly shelved.

Just before the outbreak of the First World War, there was an attack on *The Rokeby Venus*. On 10 March 1914, at ten o'clock in the morning, Mary Richardson, a militant suffragette, marched into the National Gallery with a small axe and, just before lunch-time when the attention of the two detectives who were guarding the painting was distracted, smashed the glass which covered it and slashed the canvas in a way which was absolutely devastating, with multiple gashes all the way across it. *The Times* reported that, 'The famous Rokeby Velázquez . . . was mutilated yesterday morning by the prominent militant woman suffragist Mary Richardson. She attacked the picture with a small chopper with a long narrow blade, similar to the instruments used by butchers, and in a few seconds inflicted upon it severe if not irreparable damage.' 'Slasher' Mary, as she became known, explained in a note which she sent to the Women's Social and Political Union, 'I have tried to destroy the picture of the most beautiful woman in mythological history as a protest against the Government for destroying Mrs Pankhurst, who is the most beautiful character in modern history'. She also did it, she said, to get at men who 'gaped all day' at Velázquez's nude.

When war broke out, Holroyd was extremely anxious as to what would happen to the pictures. In the event, they were removed to store, leaving only a few left in London. E.M. Forster, who was a neighbour of Holroyd in Weybridge and had been given a job in the publications department, where he kept himself busy writing reviews as well as working on a biography of Samuel Butler, described how 'if he were killed by bombs, he would die, appropriately, among second-rate masterpieces'.

At the time of the Curzon Committee, two Trustees, Alfred de Rothschild and Lord Redesdale, had taken the opportunity to write a memorandum to the Treasury as to how best to keep the Director in his place. De Rothschild detailed the occasions when the Trustees had prevented 'a great many blunders from taking place', while Lord Redesdale wrote that he had 'absolutely no personal animosity' against Holroyd, but that he regarded him as 'muddle-headed in general business while as a judge of art he is really laughed at by all those whose business – or taste – bring them in contact with questions of art'. Redesdale went on to describe why he thought the judgment of the Trustees was so much superior to that of the Director:

> The Trustees are all of them men of high position who have been connected with art from their youth up; many of them are owners of magnificent galleries of paintings, some inherited . . . They are above all suspicion of interested motives . . . it will be an evil day for the national collection if their influence and power should be lowered.

Their comments were annotated by R.N. Bromley, the relevant Treasury official, with the words 'I believe that Mr. A. de Rothschild considers Manet to be "unnecessary rubbish"'.

The differences of opinion, and artistic view, between the Director and his Trustees were particularly evident in the negotiations to acquire the group of paintings offered to the National Gallery by Hugh Lane as a gift. The Trustees continued to object to them, with Lord Redesdale producing a printed memorandum at a Trustees' meeting in which he wrote:

> The National Gallery is – and should remain – a great Temple of Art. It should open its doors to

what is highest and best: never to the productions
of a degraded craze, which, it may be hoped, will
be shortlived. I should as soon expect to hear of a
Mormon service being conducted in St Paul's Cathedral
as to see an exhibition of the works of the modern
French Art-rebels in the sacred precincts of Trafalgar
Square.

The inability of the Trustees to recognise the quality of
works by impressionist artists such as Renoir and Manet
led Hugh Lane to revise the terms of his will in favour of
Dublin, but the codicil was not witnessed, leading to half a
century of dispute with the Irish government as to where his
pictures should go when Lane drowned on the *Lusitania*,
torpedoed by a German U-boat in May 1915.

Holroyd was deeply unhappy about his poor relationship
with his Trustees. Charles Holmes, who was the Director of
the National Portrait Gallery, described his situation after
the Trustees very nearly turned down his recommendation
to buy Masaccio's *Madonna and Child* (NG 3046):

As Holroyd's troubles increased and his health
declined, our relations grew more and more intimate.
His difficulties over the exhibition of the Lane
pictures, his anxiety about the Masaccio *Madonna*
and other contested purchases, now took me almost
every day to Trafalgar Square for some informal
consultation. Though Holroyd himself kept honourable
silence, it was impossible not to be aware that matters
were handled there with little consideration for his
views or feelings. The tears which I once surprised
in the Director's eyes, as he came out from the Board
Room, were further evidence that all was not well with
him, or with the place . . .

In 1916, Holroyd resigned since he had been diagnosed as suffering from heart disease. Before his retirement in June he wrote *Some Remarks on his Office By The Retiring Director,* in which he included his suggestions for future management, prefacing them with a slightly world-weary comment that 'I make this recommendation now because, as I am retiring, I cannot be accused of a foolish thirst for power, as I might have been were I still in office' and placing on record his belief that 'I think that the machinery for the purchase of pictures, especially those of reasonable value, is clumsy and inadequate and it seriously handicaps the Gallery against other buyers'. In particular, he believed that 'a Committee is much more likely to accept a plausible second rate work than something really fine, a work requiring study, understood and appreciated by one or two members of experience but which is bound to be disagreeable to or positively disliked by others'. He died not long after.

## 10. SIR CHARLES HOLMES
### 1916–28

It was suggested that the post of Director should be offered to the well-known aesthete, Charles Ricketts, who, following the model of his friend, Sydney Cockerell, who had redecorated the Fitzwilliam Museum with carpets and flowers, fantasised that he might turn the interiors of the National Gallery into an aesthetic paradise:

> It would have been a fine end to my life to nurse the dear
> old place; to put the Italians on whitewash or grey walls,
> reframe them in the gold and azure of their period, to
> use the dimly polished walnut at times for subsidiary
> frames of drawings; to place the Venetians on brocade,
> the Flemings on brocade or stamped leather, the Dutch
> on this or on whitewash, the Spaniards in black frames
> on grey walls, the British on grey panellings, etc.; to
> group the Bellini movement together with Mantegna
> away from Veronese, etc., to give effect to certain gems,
> to give Michelangelo his mouldings, and to Rembrandt
> the frames he has painted; to efface the trade stencilling
> of the ceilings, and to slowly mould the place from a
> Board of Works aspect to that of a palace.

But, he decided, probably sensibly, that he was 'unfitted to cope with the official mind'.

The Treasury instead arranged for Charles Holmes, the Director of the National Portrait Gallery, to move next door. Holmes was a much more robust character than Holroyd and quite wily. Educated at Eton and Brasenose College, Oxford, he had worked with Ricketts and Shannon at the Vale Press, had written books on Hokusai and Constable, was himself an art critic, and had been editor of the *Burlington Magazine* before being appointed Director of the National Portrait Gallery in 1909. Although not much remembered now and less of an aesthete than Ricketts (he preferred paint on the walls to fabric), he had a distinguished period of office in which he broadened the range of the collection, encouraged its publication, and managed to circumvent his Trustees, whom he regarded as generally unhelpful.

One of Holmes's early acts as Director was to arrange for a special grant of £20,000 to allow him to attend the sale of the works of art owned by Degas in March 1918, although Maynard Keynes, who was then working in the Treasury, maintained that it was he who alerted Holmes to the sale (he was himself told about it by Duncan Grant, who had seen the catalogue of the sale in Roger Fry's Bloomsbury studio). Holmes travelled to France with his moustache shaved off, pretending to be a member of the International Financial Mission in order not to be recognised by officials from the Louvre. Keynes wrote to Vanessa Bell from Paris:

> I have secured 550,000 frs to play with; Holmes is travelling out with us and I hope we shall be able to attend the sale together. The prime object is to buy Ingres; his portrait of himself being first choice; after that the Peroneau. I think Holmes had his eye on a Greco but admits there would be another chance for this. I am fairly sure I can persuade him to go for the Delacroix 'Schwiter'. I shall try very hard on the journey out to persuade him to buy a Cézanne as a personal reward to me for having got him the money, but I think the present intention is not to buy a Cézanne; I have not yet discussed the question of Corot with him.

In the event Holmes was able to acquire three works by Ingres, including *Monsieur de Norvins* (NG 3291), and Delacroix's *Louis-Auguste Schwiter* (NG 3286) in the teeth of rival bids from the Louvre. He also acquired the fragments of Manet's *Execution of Maximilian* (NG 3294), but nothing by Cézanne, much to the disgust of Vanessa Bell who wrote 'Holmes's purchases are idiotic, considering his chances. He wouldn't hear of Cézanne and in the end didn't spend all the money, but came back with £5,000 unspent and no El Greco, which he might easily have had'. It was Keynes who acquired Cézanne's *Pommes*, which he left overnight under a hedge at the bottom of the track leading up to Charleston Farmhouse, where Clive and Vanessa Bell lived in Sussex.

Holmes's appointment coincided with the sale of more major works overseas. In 1921, the Duke of Westminster sold two classic English portraits, Gainsborough's *Blue Boy* and Reynolds's portrait *Mrs. Siddons as the Tragic Muse*, to Henry Huntington for his collection in Pasadena, California. But at least Philip Sassoon, a suave and worldly politician who was appointed a Trustee in 1921, described by Holmes as 'young, rich and clever' and like 'the hero in a novel by Disraeli', was able to persuade the Treasury to allow owners tax exemption if works of art were sold to a national collection. In August 1922, he also persuaded parliament to draw up a list of works of paramount significance which the Treasury committed themselves to buying if they were ever to come onto the open market. In September 1922, he very nearly succeeded in introducing the idea of a National Acquisitions Fund, which would, at last, have given the National Gallery purchasing power equivalent to that of major galleries overseas.

By now, the issue as to what the National Gallery was able to do in terms of modern French art was becoming highly problematic. The Trustees had been conservative about the

Impressionists, let alone the post-Impressionists. After they turned down the opportunity to borrow works by Cézanne from the Davies sisters, who had been collecting modern work adventurously in Cardiff, Samuel Courtauld, the great textiles magnate and a friend of members of the Bloomsbury Group, including Maynard Keynes and Roger Fry, established a special fund to enable the National Gallery to buy modern French pictures. This fund, which operated independently of the Boards of both the Tate Gallery and the National Gallery and, with advice from Roger Fry, made it possible at long last to assemble a proper collection of Impressionists, including Manet's *Corner of a Café-Concert* (NG 3858), Degas' *Young Spartans Exercising* (NG 3860) and *Miss La La at the Cirque Fernando* (NG 4121), Renoir's *At the Theatre (La Première Sortie)* (NG 3859), three great works by Van Gogh, *Sunflowers* (NG 3863), *Chair* (NG 3862) and *Wheatfield* (NG 3861), and, perhaps most spectacularly, Seurat's magnificently still, rather classical picture, *Bathers at Asnières* (NG 3908). It was a sensational group of paintings, which transformed the scope of the collection, all acquired in a short space of time between 1923 and 1925.

The catholic nature of Holmes's taste, which led him to take a great interest in the education of contemporary artists, is also demonstrated by the fact that, in 1924, he unsuccessfully recommended the acquisition of a collection of Moghul and Persian paintings and, in the same year, he was tough in negotiating the terms of the bequest of the Mond Collection, ensuring that it could in future be dispersed through the collection rather than being hung together in a single room at the back of the National Gallery as Mond himself had wished. In 1925, Chardin's *Young Schoolmistress* (NG 4077) and *The House of Cards* (NG 4078) were left to the Gallery under the terms of the John Webb Bequest, in 1926 the Gallery acquired *The Transfiguration* (NG 4163), a Russian icon transferred to the British Museum in the 1990s, and, in 1927, Holmes suggested the acquisition of Chinese frescoes from a London dealer named Yamanaka.

In 1927, Robert (known as Robin) Benson sold his collection *en bloc* to Joseph Duveen to be shipped to America. This was, frankly, a disaster since Benson was not only a Trustee of the National Gallery, but a founding committee member of the National Art-Collections Fund and one of the authors of the Curzon Report. A member of the family bank which was to become Kleinwort Benson, he was a discriminating collector, who had himself published a catalogue of the Holford Collection formed by his father-in-law and owned a large collection of mostly Italian paintings, which he displayed in his house off Park Lane and in Sussex. The collection was particularly strong in Sienese works, never an area of great strength for the National Gallery, including several panels from Duccio's *Maestà* which Fairfax Murray had bought for him in 1886 from a farmhouse near Siena. Duveen offered a choice of one of three pictures to the Gallery as a gift and Holmes selected Correggio's *Christ taking leave of his Mother* (NG 4255). But he was reprimanded by the Board because they felt that they could have persuaded Benson to allow them more of a choice.

In fact, Holmes's relationship with his Board of Trustees remained almost as bad as Holroyd's. Reading his autobiography, *Self and Others*, it is clear that he both resisted and resented the interference of his Trustees and, by contrast, had a good working relationship with his staff, particularly his Keeper, Charles Collins Baker. His chairman, Lord Crawford, regarded him as a 'silly little man' and wrote in his diary:

> Holmes's attitude is inexplicable in all directions –
> not merely as against myself; but as I am chairman

of the Trustees I am perhaps most affronted by this extraordinary behaviour. How does it come about that the NG has such a bad reputation for rows between the Director and his Trustees? I can only suppose because the Director is brought into the public service late in life, whereas the men at the British Museum have had years of training before reaching the high administrative posts.

# 11. SIR AUGUSTUS DANIEL
## 1928-32

Holmes retired in 1928 and was replaced by Augustus Daniel, who had himself been a Trustee, apparently appointed in 1925 because the Prime Minister, Stanley Baldwin, had known him as an undergraduate and played golf with him. He has had a bad press as Director, overshadowed by the young Kenneth Clark who succeeded him, and he is the only Director not to appear in the *Dictionary of National Biography*. But as a young man, he had travelled round Italy studying the attribution of paintings with Roger Fry, who described him in a letter to his sister, Margery, as 'very learned, helps me to do the thing more thoroughly than I otherwise should, and his keenness in tracing out hardly known artists and comparing their development is immense', while in a letter to Goldsworthy Lowes Dickinson he praised Daniel's 'terrific energy and intellectual beefiness'. While Director, the National Gallery was to make two extraordinarily important acquisitions and Daniel oversaw the beginnings of the process of professionalising the staff.

In 1929, two works of art on the so-called Paramount List came onto the market. The first was the *Wilton Diptych* (NG 4451), which had been owned by Charles I before being bought in the early eighteenth century by the eighth Earl of Pembroke and had remained at Wilton House ever since. The second was Titian's *Vendramin Family* (NG 4452), which had been bought from Sir Anthony van Dyck by the tenth Earl of Northumberland in 1645 and was being sold by the eighth Duke. The government, with Winston Churchill as Chancellor of the Exchequer, paid half the price of both pictures, while the rest was raised from the National Art-Collections Fund and private individuals, including Courtauld and Duveen. As William Ormsby-Gore stated in a debate in the House of Commons,

> It is important that this country, for artistic reasons, should retain these exceptional works. After all the National Gallery is used by artists and students and also appeals to a far wider circle, and there is an enormous number of people to whom really great works of art are a source of spiritual enjoyment which cannot be assessed in pounds, shilling and pence. So long as we are a great and wealthy nation it ought to be our duty to provide the public and visitors to the country with the finest works of art for their spiritual refreshment, education and enjoyment, and I am sure the Government and the Trustees are fortunate in having acquired this year two of the outstanding works of art which will henceforward be amongst the richest treasures of our already great collection.

Previously, the Directors had invariably been painters. There was a slight air of amateurism about the ways in which even the Keepers studied and interpreted the collection, as is evident in the work of Charles Collins Baker, who was described in his obituary as belonging to 'the last great age of the self-taught scholar in England, before it was permissible to call oneself an art historian, and *Lely and the Stuart Portrait Painters*, [published in] 1912, achieved with no greater mechanical aid than a bicycle, is the last great scholarly monument of that generation'.

But in the early 1930s the discipline of art history was being professionalised with the foundation of the Courtauld Institute in 1931 and the arrival of the Warburg Institute from Hamburg in 1933. In 1929, Ellis Waterhouse was appointed as an Assistant Keeper. It was already evident that he was going to be a brilliant scholar: a precocious schoolboy with a first class degree from Oxford, he came to the National Gallery by way of Princeton where he had been a Commonwealth Fund Fellow and had worked under the art historian, Frank Mather, on El Greco. Having been at Princeton, he was knowledgeable about current German and American art historical scholarship. He was shocked by the amateurishness of his colleagues at the National Gallery and resigned in a huff in 1933 in order to move to Rome where he wrote his pioneering study of *Baroque Painting in Rome* as librarian to the British School.

In 1930, Martin Davies joined the staff, initially as an unpaid *attaché* and from 1932 as Assistant Keeper, and, like Waterhouse, he helped to pioneer a much more scholarly and systematic approach to the study of the works of art under his care, announcing in the *Burlington Magazine* in 1937 a new approach to cataloguing. 'A proposed re-edition of the National Gallery catalogues' was expected 'to embody a scholarship more ample and more up-to-date [which] forced the staff to consider many difficult problems'. This was an understatement: Davies essentially devoted his life to the patient and most scrupulous examination of works of art, based on their documentation.

The fact that Augustus Daniel had himself been a Trustee did not protect him from what he described as 'the tyranny and malignancy' of the Board. Its poisonous atmosphere led to the departure of W.G. Constable, the Deputy Director, to be Director of the newly established Courtauld Institute and of Charles Collins Baker, the Keeper, to the Huntington Library in California. Collins Baker wrote a letter to Max Ferrand, the Director of the Huntington Library, in which he made clear his feelings towards the Board of Trustees:

We have been hearing on the radio, a series of public men expounding 'What I would do with the World if I were a Dictator'. If I were Dictator, I would see to it that the technical experts – scientists, scholars, artists, engineers, soldiers, etc. etc., were freed from the interference of a false aristocracy – whether of caste or wealth. No peer should, because he was a peer, patronize or bully or direct scholars who knew their job, nor exercise a supremacy of caste. Nor should a millionaire exercise a supremacy of wealth over the architect or scholar.

In 1932, Augustus Daniel, too, decided not to seek re-appointment, writing to Evan Charteris, one of his Trustees, that 'I have suffered so much for the last two years that I shall be only too thankful for a change'.

## 12. SIR KENNETH CLARK
### 1934–45

The vacancy led to the appointment in January 1934 of one of the most remarkable of the National Gallery's Directors, Kenneth Clark, the young scion of an immensely wealthy Glasgow textile family, educated at Winchester and Trinity College, Oxford, a student of Bernard Berenson at *I Tatti* and author of a pioneering study of the Gothic Revival. In 1930, on returning from Italy, Clark had been one of the organisers of the great exhibition of Italian Art at Burlington House, made possible by Mussolini's fascist government, and in 1931 he was appointed Keeper at the Ashmolean. Although temperamentally rather shy and regarded by his staff as arrogant, Clark had the advantage of being at ease with the Trustees, with a beautiful wife, a house in Portland Place, and very substantial private means. At the time of his appointment, he was only thirty-one.

It has become common for art historians to be dismissive of Clark's qualifications, as indeed were his colleagues at the National Gallery, as if he was too rich, too successful, and too worldly to be properly regarded as a scholar. But he was extremely knowledgeable and had a good eye, as well as being a serious student of Leonardo and having much more serious academic qualifications than most of his predecessors. He has described his arrival at the National Gallery in his autobiography, *Another Part of the Wood*:

> I entered it, on the first of January, 1934, with rather
> less than my usual confidence. The door seemed very
> large, and at the end of the corridor leading to my room

was the head of a Mantegna cast in bronze, scowling
contemptuously at those who were impudent enough
to question authority. I did not know any of the staff
and obviously my first duty was to present myself to
my second in command, known as the Keeper. During
the troubles before my appointment the Treasury had
innocently appointed as Keeper someone from outside
the museum world, an elderly inspector of education
named Glasgow, who, in his youth, had published a
book of drawings of Wadham College. I found him an
affable and tolerant man, but when I asked him about
his colleagues his face fell.

This passage perfectly conveys Clark's attitude to the
National Gallery as somewhere which he looked back on as
alien to his refined scholarly and artistic sensibility and which
he regarded in retrospect with a somewhat sardonic eye, not
helped by the fact that nearly all his staff had detested him.

Wanting to make his mark when he arrived, Clark did so by
re-hanging the collection in such a way as to earn the esteem
of his Bloomsbury friends, moving Van Dyck's *Charles I on
Horseback* because it apparently overwhelmed the British
display in Room XXV (now Room 9) and including a much
stronger representation of work by Manet and Cézanne, then
still regarded as dangerously modern. As Helen Anrep wrote
to him on 20 March 1935

At last I got a happy free afternoon to go to the
National Gallery. I knew I would be glad to be there
and looking at pictures again but I had no notion how
exquisite and exciting it would be with your hanging –
It isn't that you have improved things, that this or that
picture looks better. It's a completely new Gallery –
You have so changed the tenor and mood that one sees

an old picture from such a different angle with such
new associations that it is, if not a new picture, or new
aspect of that artist – The whole place seems full of a
new gaiety and fragrance and the individuality of minor
men [has] acquired such a clear tone.

She was able to report that Roger (i.e. Roger Fry) would
have been thrilled.

Clark had complete confidence in his ability to hang
according to the judgment of his eye – an ability which he
felt he had been born with and was conferred by his aesthetic
judgment, which he always regarded as at least as important
to the understanding and appreciation of works of art as
knowledge of their history:

> From childhood onwards hanging pictures has been my
> favourite occupation. It has been a substitute for being
> a painter and a concrete illustration of my feelings as a
> critic. It is a curious art. One never knows what pictures
> are going to say to one another till they meet. Like two
> placid babies passing each other in their prams, they
> may either stretch out their arms in longing or scream
> with rage. People who hang galleries 'on paper', with
> measured squares representing the pictures, have never
> heard those cries of love or hate.

In other words, Clark's approach to the hanging of paintings was intuitive, based on the visual relationship between
works of art and their formal values, rather than on a more
strictly logical or historical sequence. His pleasure was akin
to that of treating it as a semi-private collection and the
comment about people who hang galleries 'on paper' was
an implied criticism of the methods of his successor, Philip
Hendy, who was known to have organised his hang by

working with little, scaled-down reproductions of the paintings on graph paper.

In 1934, Clark appointed Philip Pouncey as curator, the only member of staff with whom he subsequently claimed any intellectual sympathy and who went on to develop extraordinary skills of connoisseurship, which he devoted after the Second World War to the study of Italian drawings in the British Museum. During the same period, Denis Mahon was working in the library, undertaking the research which led to him being one of the greatest scholars, as well as collectors, of Italian Baroque painting. And, John Pope-Hennessy, the future Director of the Victoria and Albert Museum, apparently 'curried favour with Kenneth Clark in the 1930s to the extent of being taken on as an unpaid *attaché*', as was Benedict Nicolson, future editor of the *Burlington Magazine* and the son of Harold Nicolson and Vita Sackville-West. Pope-Hennessy's famously imperious manner upset the staff so much that they threatened to rebel and, according to Cecil Gould, a later curator, Pope-Hennessy 'not surprisingly clashed with Martin Davies, who had snubbed him (some feat) and who disapproved of his reliance on stylistic criticism in preference to documentary evidence'.

For the first time, the Gallery also employed a professional conservator as a member of its professional staff, Helmut Ruhemann from Germany, and established a scientific laboratory through the appointment of Ian Rawlins, a physicist who had trained at the Universities of Cambridge and Marburg.

Almost as soon as Ruhemann had started working at the National Gallery, controversy erupted over his cleaning of Velázquez's *Philip IV of Spain in Brown and Silver*. The battle lines were drawn up with Clark supporting Ruhemann and artist members of the Royal Academy opposed. On the one side, Clark believed that it was essential to get back, as far as possible, to the original intention of the artist, by the removal of later layers of discoloured varnish. Clark declared that 'the picture was cleaned in the simplest and most conservative way by one of the most reputable living cleaners'. On the other side, his critics believed that the picture looked 'as if it might have been painted today, in preparation for next year's Academy'. They suggested the establishment of a Society for the Protection of Old Masters.

Clark's other innovations included introducing electric light into the galleries in 1934, opening in the evening until 8p.m. in order to give 'the workaday public increased facilities for enjoyment and study', early evening public lectures in a first-floor lecture room, and the use of a PR Agency called 'Echoes', which was used to advertise Clark's new hangs and the 'picture of the week', an idea which he borrowed from the V&A. Perhaps most importantly in terms of the future audience for the National Gallery, just before the Second World War he opened a 'New Exhibition Room', which was intended to house temporary exhibitions, much smaller and more low-key than those which were attracting large numbers to the Royal Academy. Two were held before the start of the War, the first on depictions of classical antiquity in Renaissance painting organised by Rudolph Wittkower, the librarian of the Warburg Institute, the second on portraiture.

But, of course, what Clark loved best was making acquisitions, not only for the National Gallery but also works by Cézanne, Renoir and Picasso for himself. In 1934, the Gallery acquired Bosch's *Christ Mocked (The Crowning with Thorns)* (NG 4744), Hogarth's charming *The Graham Children* (NG 4756) and Sassetta's *Scenes from the Life of St Francis* (NG 4757–63), which he bought from Duveen, who was by now (quite improperly) himself a Trustee.

In 1935, Clark was able to make two brilliant acquisitions – Rubens's *The Watering Place* (NG 4815), which he bought from the Duke of Buccleuch, and Ingres' fine portrait of

*Madame Moitessier* (NG 4821), strengthening the Gallery's early nineteenth-century holdings. But, in 1937, he slipped up, buying four small panels as Giorgiones (they were correctly attributed by Philip Pouncey to Andrea Previtali (NG 4884)) for £14,000 against the advice of his curators, who never forgave him and were subsequently to quarrel with him so badly that Lord Balniel, the chairman of Trustees, was forced to investigate, discovering that, led by Martin Davies, they had apparently locked Clark out of the library, objecting to his policy of popularisation, when they believed that 'the prestige of the Gallery could only be enhanced by its becoming an institute of scholarship' and, according to Clark himself, especially disliking his taste in ties.

Clark's innovations were brought to a premature end by the threat of war and the need to evacuate the pictures to safe accommodation in north Wales. The Trustees hatched a plan to ship the pictures to Canada, but Clark prevented this proposal, writing to Winston Churchill who instantly forbade it. Nearly the entire collection was instead packed into crates and moved by railway to three locations – the National Library of Wales in Aberystwyth, the Prichard-Jones Hall at the University College of North Wales in Bangor and the garage of Penrhyn Castle, a neo-Norman country house outside Bangor. By 3 September 1939, Clark was able to report to the Treasury that

> The evacuation of all the pictures from the Gallery
> is now complete. All pictures of any value had been
> removed before the weekend. Yesterday and today we
> have sent off the first two containers of books from the
> library as well as two containers with some mediocre
> pictures which seemed just worth saving. I have decided
> to leave about twenty-five pictures which cannot under
> any circumstances be considered of interest or value.

Unfortunately, the collection was not safe in Penrhyn Castle, because, according to Martin Davies, the Assistant Keeper in charge, 'the owner is celebrating the war by being fairly constantly drunk'. Samuel Courtauld, chairman of Trustees, ordered the staff to seek underground storage in a nearby slate quarry and, in July 1940, Ian Rawlins was able to report that he had found the ideal place deep underground in Manod Quarry on the hillside above Blaenau Ffestiniog. During the following year, the space was made safe and the pictures were moved there in August 1941. Some of the staff lived in a farmhouse nearby, including Martin Davies, who was able to undertake much of the research for his great catalogue of the early Italian collection (he seems to have relished having an opportunity of having the collection to himself without the interference of the public), and Helmut Ruhemann, who was able to undertake conservation work undisturbed by prying eyes.

While the pictures were underground in north Wales, the National Gallery itself was used for daily concerts from Monday to Friday organised by Myra Hess, a formidably energetic professional pianist, who travelled by tube every day from Hampstead. The first was held under the dome of the Barry Rooms at 1pm on Tuesday 10 October 1939. 850 people paid one shilling for admission, although there was space for only 500. According to Clark, the audience consisted of 'All sorts. Young and old, smart and shabby, Tommies in uniform with their tin hats strapped on, old ladies with their ear trumpets, musical students, civil servants, office boys, busy public men, all sorts had come. . . .'

In March 1940, Lillian Browse, a young art dealer who had met Clark in Coventry, organised *British Painting since Whistler*, the first of a series of exhibitions, which were likewise successful in lifting the morale of those left in the capital during a period of heavy bombing. There was a feeling that the National Gallery was a bastion of civilisation representing the values for which the war was being fought. Later in 1940, rooms were made available to the War Artist's Advisory Committee, of which Kenneth Clark was chairman and, in November 1940, there was an exhibition of the drawings of Augustus John, with exhibitions in 1941 of the work of Whistler and Sickert. The following year, John Betjeman, press attaché to the Ambassador in Dublin and an old friend of Kenneth Clark, suggested an exhibition devoted to the work of Jack Yeats, whose work was shown alongside that of Sir William Nicholson. The final exhibition in the series was of *Nineteenth-Century French Painting.* As Lillian Browse described it in her autobiography, *The Duchess of Cork Street*

> The complete exhibition, entitled *Nineteenth-Century French Painting* was of such high quality that by any standards, even those of more propitious times, it was considered a 'knock-out' with the press reporting 'the most successful art exhibition ever held in London . . . drawing thirty-seven thousand people in thirty days' – and this took place at the height of the war.

But the period of the war is best remembered for the monthly exhibition of a single picture brought back specially from the quarries in north Wales and displayed in the Barry Rooms where the daily concerts were held. This derived from a suggestion by Charles Wheeler, the sculptor, in a letter to *The Times* on 1 January 1942:

> Because London's face is scarred and bruised these days we need more than ever to see beautiful things. Like many another one hungry for aesthetic refreshment, I would welcome the opportunity of seeing a few of the

hundreds of the nation's masterpieces now stored in a
safe place. Would the trustees of the National Gallery
consider whether it were not wise and well to risk one
picture for exhibition each week? Arrangements could
be made to transfer it quickly to a strong room in case
of an alert. Music-lovers are not denied their Beethoven,
but picture-lovers are denied their Rembrandts just at a
time when such beauty is most potent for good. I know
the risk, but I believe it would be worth it.

The first picture shown was Rembrandt's portrait of
*Margaretha Trip* (NG 5282), which had been presented by
the National Art-Collections Fund in 1941 (it came from
the collection of Lord Crawford, the chairman of Trustees)
and was seen by large crowds 'hungry for aesthetic nourish-
ment'. The next was Titian's *Noli Me Tangere* (NG 270) in
March 1942. In September 1943, 35,000 people came to see
Velázquez's *Rokeby Venus*.

The use of the National Gallery during the Second World
War for concerts and cups of coffee and exhibitions of modern
British art, as well as for the opportunity to see a single great
work of art as a reminder of why the war was being fought,
changed the relationship of the Gallery to its public. Instead
of being somewhere simply for the solitary contemplation of
works of art, it was transformed into a place of mass democratic culture. As the *Observer* declared at the end of the
war

The National Gallery is far more genuinely a national
possession than ever before. It has a new quality most
rare in such places. It seems to be full of people actually
liking things . . . It is easy to invent a sneer at a policy
which makes pictures popular by easing the strain with
sandwiches and Mozart at lunchtime. But surely an Art

Gallery should be a home of all the arts, even that of making a good cup of coffee.

No sooner had the Second World War ended than Kenneth Clark decided to resign in order to concentrate on his writing. He knew that he was not much loved by his staff, he himself felt that he lacked the common touch, and he had done so many other things during the war, including working for the Central Office of Information, that he probably did not want to return to the relatively boring routine of being a Museum Director.

# 13. SIR PHILIP HENDY
## 1945–68

The Trustees appointed Philip Hendy, the ambitious, capable but somewhat rebarbative Director of the Leeds City Art Galleries, who, like Clark, greatly admired the work of contemporary British artists like Henry Moore (he was to hang a Calder mobile in his house in Oxfordshire and had resigned his former post at the Museum of Fine Arts in Boston after being criticised for buying Matisse's *Carmelina*), but, unlike Clark, disapproved of the rich on political grounds and, five years after his appointment, narrowly escaped being dismissed by his Board.

Hendy faced the task of re-hanging the collection, patching up the bomb-damaged building, and returning to normal in a climate of post-war austerity, since by the end of the war, the National Gallery presented a sorry sight:

> All the skylights in all the exhibition rooms had been
> damaged by shrapnel. None of them had preserved
> more than about a quarter of their glass. The missing
> areas had been boarded over. Naturally no redecoration
> had been done since before the war – in most cases
> long before it. The ancient Lincrusta wallpapers, with
> their patterns in relief, which featured in most of the
> rooms, were now heavily stained where water had come
> through the holes in the roof.

Hendy explained the logic of how he hung the collection in his first Annual Report. He starts with the arrangement of the rooms:

In its present form, truncated but more symmetrical than before, the Gallery has as its centre no longer in Room I but in the Dome. In fact the Dome has come to dominate the building. The size and importance of the Italian altarpieces there have been increased; but I think I have made a mistake in following tradition and putting the finest of the large early Renaissance pictures in Room I, and not in the four rooms which radiate from the Dome. There they would support the altarpieces and make a still stronger centre, as well as filling the height of the rooms better.

Here one sees an incoming Director grappling with the issues of the architecture of the building and what looks best where. Like Clark, Hendy believed that the look of the collection was at least as important as its intellectual logic. He went on to describe how

The traditional grouping by schools has been largely maintained; but a good many exceptions have been made, partly for the sake of a more harmonious and stimulating ensemble and partly for the sake of historical truth, to show that the spirit of the time is usually more important than national boundaries, and that ideas can transcend both.

The wording of Hendy's statement indicates the duality of his concern: for the look of the paintings on the one hand, influenced by his modernist aesthetic; and, on the other hand, by the intellectual logic of following the *zeitgeist* rather than a layout dominated by national schools.

Hendy was not only interested in the look of the collection, but also in its environmental conditions, being a passionate believer in the benefits of an understanding of science to the display of the collection. He was responsible for installing air conditioning, following the experience of monitoring the stable, atmospheric conditions of the quarries in which the pictures had been stored during the Second World War. This, in turn, made it possible to take the glass off the pictures in order to allow for a more immediate and more intimate experience of their picture surface – glass had previously been necessary as a protection from soot. In 1947, damask was introduced as a background to the pictures, not because of its aesthetic qualities, but because it was a first step towards the control of relative humidity. Apparently 'by taking the moisture from humid air and giving it out when the air is dry, [damask] does much to keep the atmosphere stable. It has other practical virtues, of which the greatest, in view of the undesirability of frequently changing Rooms for redecoration, is its relative permanence'.

Hendy is remembered as being authoritarian in the way he hung pictures, reluctant, at least in his early years as Director, to delegate the responsibility to his Keeper and Assistant Keepers. Perhaps surprisingly, his attitude to the hanging of the collection was the subject of debate in the House of Lords where, in 1954, Lord Strabolgi deplored the fact that 'There is a tendency at the National Gallery to concentrate too much on what I may call "window-dressing" for the benefit mainly of the ordinary visitor' and Lord Methuen, a former Trustee and owner of Corsham Court, agreed, regarding it as a betrayal of the old and well-tried policy of getting and keeping together a collection of pictures 'to illustrate the history of Western art as fully as possible'. There is, of course, a certain historical irony that, at this period, it was the Trustees was wanted a historical approach to display, while the Director wanted it to be more theatrical, since, during the nineteenth century, it had been the other way round.

Alongside his preoccupation with the display of the collection, Hendy had to grapple with the report of the so-called Massey committee, which met to consider the constitutional relationship between the National Gallery and the Tate Gallery. When the Tate Gallery split from the National Gallery in 1917 and was given the remit for modern foreign painting as well as British, the Director of the National Gallery was an *ex officio* Tate Trustee, as were three of the National Gallery Trustees, and the Tate Gallery did not have a separate purchase grant. Vincent Massey, the Canadian High Commissioner, was a Trustee of both institutions and so was well placed to examine their relationship. He recommended a system whereby works of art held by the Tate could, in due course, be 'promoted' to the National Gallery, which was expected to be the institution for works of pre-eminent quality. In other words, the Tate was expected to try to be comprehensive in its coverage of modern art, whereas the National Gallery could afford to be – and was expected to be – much more rigorously selective:

> It is obvious that, with the passage of time, certain pictures acquired by the Tate will eventually fall within the scope of the National Gallery and that some, though not all, of these should properly be 'promoted' for exhibition at the senior institution. The National Gallery is not simply a collection of Old Masters, but aims primarily at providing the finest possible selection of their works, at providing, in fact, a gallery of masterpieces rather than an historical collection, and it would be out of the question that pictures should be transferred for exhibition from the Tate to Trafalgar Square merely upon attaining an age that disqualified them from further exhibition at Millbank.

Another issue that Hendy was expected to deal with was what to do about the collection of the great oil magnate, Calouste Gulbenkian. Gulbenkian had been assiduously courted in the pre-war period by Clark, who blamed Hendy for not securing the collection for the nation after the war, although it cannot have helped that Gulbenkian had been regarded as an enemy alien during the war, had been closely associated with the Vichy government, and was seeking a wholly new building for his collection which would have totally contravened the convention that new acquisitions, including those bequeathed by a single individual such as Ludwig Mond, should be integrated into the collection as a whole.

A further issue which preoccupied Hendy was conservation, about which he was said to have had a bee in his bonnet. He decided to celebrate the work which had been done in cleaning seventy pictures during the war by holding 'An Exhibition of Cleaned Pictures' in October 1947. He probably knew that it was going to shock, because he wrote in the accompanying catalogue 'When pictures are presented together hung in rows, room after room, any one that is exceptional in tone or in degree of individual expression is almost bound to shock'. But he believed that 'There can be no deep understanding of old pictures without a knowledge of their state, of how much has to be allowed for the distortions caused by old varnishes, by damages and by unsuitable restorations'.

At the same time, Hendy arranged for 'a Committee of Confidential Inquiry into the Cleaning and the Care of Pictures in The National Gallery' to report on the Gallery's methods of conservation. It was chaired by J.R. Weaver, the President of Trinity College, Oxford, and included George Stout of the Fogg Art Museum in Harvard and Paul Coremans of the Belgian National Museums. As Cecil Gould was to comment in his unpublished autobiography, 'as both of these were restorers and had been chosen by Hendy as being likely to agree with him the dice were loaded in his favour'.

Meanwhile, there were a surprising number of acquisitions owing to cheap prices in the art market after the war, including, in 1945, Poussin's *The Adoration of the Golden Calf* (NG 5597), acquired from Lord Radnor's collection at Longford Castle. Two years later, in 1947, another great Poussin, the *Landscape with a Man killed by a Snake* (NG 5763) was acquired for only £6,500 from the collection of Sir Watkin Williams-Wynn.

In 1952, a bill was introduced to parliament to enact the recommendations of the Massey Committee. But the exact relationship between the National Gallery and the Tate was left studiously ambiguous:

> We have considered carefully the formula proposed by the Massey Committee for drawing a line between the collections at the Tate Gallery and the National Gallery. We do not believe that any fixed formula will serve the purpose. What matters is not the date at which a picture is painted nor the date of the artist's birth, but the rise of new ideas and new schools. The division of pictures now, and the time for transfer of any picture or group of pictures, from one collection to the other, must be matters of judgment and must have regard to the practical possibilities of hanging.

The two galleries eventually went their separate ways in 1955 with a division of the collection which was based on where the pictures were at the time and which, not surprisingly, reflected the views and tastes of the 1950s. A small selection of the greatest British pictures remained in Trafalgar Square, but these were a manifestation of a view of British art which did not really recognise eighteenth-century painters outside the canon of Hogarth, Reynolds and Gainsborough and, in the nineteenth century, not much besides Constable and Turner, and even these artists were represented by their grand exhibition works rather than their more lively oil sketches, some of which Kenneth Clark had discovered rolled up in the basement during the war. No Pre-Raphaelites stayed and nor did the three great Whistlers – *Symphony in White, No. 2: The Little White Girl* (Tate N03418), *Nocturne: Blue and Silver – Cremorne Lights* (Tate N03420) and *Nocturne: Black and Gold – The Fire Wheel* (Tate N03419) – which had been bequeathed by the artist, Arthur Studd, in 1919 with the stipulation that they were 'not to be hung in the Tate Gallery or anywhere else except the National Gallery'. These issues as to what should be displayed where remained issues of debate for a long time afterwards and, by 1957, Hendy was quarrelling with Sir John Rothenstein as to where the boundary should be for modern pictures:

I personally favour a principle and date-line and a period which can be easily grasped and remembered. As principles I suggest that all artists should become N.G. graduates when they are 100 years old, and that the graduation ceremony takes place every ten years. A century and a decade are ideas simple enough for the public to grasp and remember, and comfortable enough for those in the Galleries who have to cope with the practical results. Thus in this year of grace the birth-date beyond which no artist should have failed to graduate to the National Gallery would be 1850. However, transfers would occur only every 10 years, and therefore nothing would be done until 1960, when Cézanne (b. 1839), Monet (1840), Renoir (1841) and others would automatically cease to be housed at the Tate.

Looking at the acquisitions during the 1950s, they, too, are inevitably representative of the taste of the time. Hendy was keen on early Italian paintings and acquired two panels thought to be by Masolino, one of which, the *Saint Jerome and John the Baptist* (NG 5962), has been re-attributed to Masaccio, and, in 1959, Uccello's *Saint George and the Dragon* (NG 6294) from the Lanckoroński Collection in Vienna, a picture whose attribution was, and remains, a matter of scholarly dispute. He was also keen on nineteenth-century French painting and acquired Courbet's *Still Life with Apples and a Pomegranate* (NG 5983) and Renoir's *A Nymph by a Stream* (NG 5982) in 1951, Cézanne's *An Old Woman with a Rosary* (NG 6195) in 1953, Renoir's *Moulin Huet Bay, Guernsey* (NG 6204) in 1954 and Delacroix's *Ovid among the Scythians* (NG 6262) in 1956. He campaigned vigorously in favour of the National Gallery buying modern French painting and, in 1960, published an article in the *Listener* in which he claimed

> Cézanne belongs to the great tradition of the past. In the
> context of the twentieth century he is an 'Old Master'.
> His place is in the National Gallery. And there is the
> tragedy. It played a leading part in bringing back into
> public esteem, on to a level with Raphael and Titian and
> Rubens, the great masters of the earlier Renaissance
> . . . But it has not been equally perspicacious at the other
> end of the history of painting.

Meanwhile, in spite of the separation of the Tate, the National Gallery itself continued to acquire major British paintings: Reynolds's portrait of one of the great soldiers of the American Revolution, *Colonel Tarleton* (NG 5984) in 1951, two Richard Wilsons in 1954, and Gainsborough's *Morning Walk* (NG 6209), which was bought from Victor

Rothschild, the eminent zoologist, bibliophile and former member of MI5, in 1955. In March 1960, Gainsborough's *Mr. and Mrs. Andrews* (NG 6301) came onto the market, sold by direct descendants of the sitters to Agnew's and then to the National Gallery. It was representative of a shift in post-war taste in British art away from the grand swagger portraits, which had been so much admired by American collectors in the 1920s, towards the smaller and more finicky, domestic paintings of Gainsborough's earlier career, which appealed to a new interest in intimacy and realism.

More serious than the possible loss of *Mr. and Mrs. Andrews* was the announcement in March 1962 that the Royal Academy was proposing to sell Leonardo's *Virgin and Child with St Anne and St John the Baptist* (NG 6337), the so-called Leonardo Cartoon, for £800,000. Although it was technically a drawing, and so might have been thought to belong in the British Museum, Lord Crawford, as former chairman of Trustees, now chairman of the National Art-Collections Fund, led a vigorous and successful campaign to acquire it. He heard about the sale while waiting in Madrid Airport and was able to persuade the Treasury to second two civil servants to help alongside ten paid staff and fifty volunteers, who co-ordinated the campaign and sent free posters to every school in the country. It was acquired in July 1962 with a special grant of £350,000 from the Civil Contingencies Fund.

During his twenty-two years as Director, Hendy is remembered as having been slightly timid in his approach to acquisitions, hampered by post-war austerity and a belief that the great period when one could buy works of art relatively cheaply was now over. But he made at least two more major acquisitions before his retirement in 1967. In 1961, the Gallery acquired Goya's portrait of the *Duke of Wellington* (NG 6322), which was stolen not long afterwards by a thief who hid in the gentlemen's lavatory after closing time and managed to get out through a window as a protest at the cost of television licences for old age pensioners, pestering the Director with letters written in purple ink. It was recovered in May 1965 in the lost property office of Birmingham New Street station. In 1964, Cézanne's magnificent *Bathers* (NG 6359) was acquired despite it being regarded as being extremely expensive and assumed to be destined for the Louvre.

Hendy remained a passionate believer in the virtues of modern methods of conservation: perhaps slightly too passionate, because he was quite happy to adopt a combative attitude to those, including Ernst Gombrich and Otto Kurz of the Warburg Institute, who criticised him, devoting most of the *Annual Report January 1960–May 1962* to a long and robust defence of the cleaning of Titian's *Noli Me Tangere*.

In fact, by far the greatest controversy erupted in 1969 with the unveiling of the Titian's newly cleaned *Bacchus and Ariadne*, which emerged from the studio, where it had been cleaned in too great haste by Arthur Lucas, who had replaced Ruhemann as chief restorer, and looked as if it was newly painted, too pristine for the taste of most art historians, and the largely repainted sky too blue. Once again, it was clear that there are radical differences of opinion between those who believe that it is the responsibility of the professional conservator to return a picture as far as possible to what are presumed to be the original intentions of the artist and those who prefer a more tentative approach and the soothing, if inaccurate, effect of the passage of time.

## 14. SIR MARTIN DAVIES
### 1968–74

In 1968, Hendy was succeeded for a few years by Martin Davies, a fine if somewhat dry scholar, who had set a new standard in the post-war cataloguing of the collection, but an austere bachelor, who always carried a string bag filled with library books and oranges. He is described very accurately in his entry in the *Dictionary of National Biography* as 'a civil servant in the old mould – a precise, fastidious, and unobtrusive administrator'. He was obviously totally out of sympathy with the mood of the late 1960s, setting out a course for the National Gallery that it should keep itself aloof from vulgar populism. His colleagues apparently knew him as 'Dry Martini' and he was described by Erwin Panofsky, the great German art historian, as 'obviously descended from a long line of unmarried English clergymen'.

Davies announced his attitude to display in the Trustees' Annual Report for the period January 1969–December 1970:

A seemingly attractive option is that the National
Gallery need not seek to excel in display techniques; the
pictures of the Collection are competent to have their
say. Yet permitting that is a display technique: of not
scrambling the message.

This seems straightforward, but it is clear how culturally specific it is when it goes on to say:

Variety of wall-coverings is considered desirable.
Changes may be noticed by visitors in the choice

for certain Rooms of material that is not damask,
and is without a pattern conspicuously woven in . . .
Much work to reduce adverse effects from the heavy
architecture is needed.

This passage helps to confirm that the orthodoxy of the
time was minimal information – 'allowing the pictures to
have their say' – although there was some recognition, at least
on the part of Michael Levey when he was Keeper, that there
was public demand for more information about the collection
since he arranged for so-called 'room bats' to be available, as
in historic churches. There was a general determination to get
away from the characteristics of a historic hang by abolishing
damask and disguising the Victorian architecture, which was
then regarded as heavy, distracting and over-ornate.

Davies had to face a number of tough tests. The first
was the sale in 1969 of Tiepolo's extremely beautiful ceiling painting, *An Allegory with Venus and Time* (NG 6387)
which hung in the United Arab Embassy in Curzon Street.
This was successfully acquired. The second was the possibility of acquiring Velázquez's portrait of his servant, *Juan de
Pareja*, which was sold by Lord Radnor at Christie's in 1970
for £2,320,000, then a record price. The Export Reviewing
Committee, which had been set up after the Second World
War to help prevent the export of works of art, refused an
export licence for three months in order to give the National
Gallery a chance to raise the necessary funds. It was impossible. The picture went instead to the Metropolitan Museum
in New York. The failure to acquire such a great painting
perhaps prepared the ground for the successful public appeal
to save Titian's *Death of Actaeon* (NG 6420), which had
been sold by Lord Harewood in June 1971 and bought by
John Paul Getty in California, but was refused an export
licence. In 1972, the Gallery was also able to acquire Henri

(le Douanier) Rousseau's *The Tropical Storm with a Tiger* (NG 6421), bought by Walter Annenberg who, when he discovered that the National Gallery wanted it, gave a very large sum to help.

# 15. SIR MICHAEL LEVEY
## 1974–86

In 1974 Davies was succeeded by Michael Levey – a brilliantly intelligent writer and scholar, who had joined the staff of the Gallery in 1951, had been Slade Professor in Cambridge, and had already published a number of works of general art history, including *Painting in Eighteenth-century Venice* in 1959 and a beautifully written, more general book on the *Early Renaissance*, alongside his National Gallery catalogues of the Later Italian and German Schools. He was known as a figure of the 1960s, highly sociable, extremely democratic, a vegetarian with a taste for purple corduroy. He was married to the novelist, Bridget Brophy, and had slightly scandalised the Trustees by appearing in a colour supplement which alluded to the fact that his fourteen-year old daughter had a live-in lover; but now the balance of authority between the Director and his Trustees was somewhat different, particularly during the time that John Hale was chairman, a chain-smoking Professor of Italian at London University who admired Levey's intellect and was regarded by his fellow Trustees as being too deferential to the views of his Director.

Levey's first preoccupation was with the opening of the new north galleries by the Queen on 9 June 1975. They had been designed in a style of post-war brutalism. The annual report for the period 1973 to 1975 shows the building in all its newly opened glory with a grand, polygonal structure advertising the Gallery on the pavement on Orange Street and celebrating its various amenities, including a newly opened smoking room. In 1976, the basic guide was re-written by

Homan Potterton to accommodate the change to the plan of the gallery by the opening of these galleries, which he described as 'a model of discretion and reticence in comparison to the grandeur of the Victorian interiors'.

It had originally been planned that the northern extension should be opened with an exhibition of German Art, but, when this proved impossible, it was devoted instead to an exhibition titled *The Rival of Nature – Renaissance Painting in its Context*, which consisted mainly of paintings from the Gallery's own collection, enhanced by displays of works in other media lent by the British Museum, the Royal Collection and the V&A. There were 350,000 visitors, a remarkable number and more than for most exhibitions today. An exhibition of Dutch Art, intended to 'explore the richness and diversity of the art produced in Holland in the seventeenth century' was mounted in 1976. It was seen by nearly half a million people.

The northern extension also demonstrated Levey's preoccupation with museum education. He established an education department under Alistair Smith, one of the Gallery's Assistant Keepers, and the extension included a small cinema and a seminar room 'where advanced students can withdraw to discuss what they have seen'. Christmas activities were extended to include quizzes and jigsaw puzzles, with a competition of drawings judged by John Piper. From this point onwards, it is clear that educational activities were increasingly at the heart of the Gallery's view of its responsibilities, including special courses for teachers, collaboration with the Open University and the extra-mural department of London University, and guided tours for visitors.

Not long after Levey became Director, the vexed issue of the relationship with the Tate once again became a topic of debate between the two institutions. Levey wrote down his views in an unpublished memorandum:

A general feeling exists that the N.G. Collection
gradually tails off or fades away after 1800. This is
broadly true, unfortunately. It gives to the Gallery a
quite un-wished for air of old-fashionedness around our
concept of what constitutes great European painting
. . . The supreme distinction of the National Gallery
Collection lies in the fact that it is among the most
balanced of all fine representations of European painting
in the world. Particularly ironic therefore would it be for
us to go on limping, as it were, and handicapped by some
notional date of exclusion when we come to great art
that long ago ceased to be modern, by artists no longer
alive, whose reputations are not in doubt, and which
having been absorbed into the tradition of European
painting should be found in the Gallery whose task it is
to represent that tradition at its finest.

Levey embarked on an ambitious programme of early
twentieth-century acquisitions, including Klimt's *Portrait of
Hermine Gallia* (NG 6434), bought in 1976, Odilon Redon's
*Ophelia among Flowers* (NG 6438) in 1977 and, most dra-
matically, Picasso's *Fruit, Bottle and Violin* (NG 6449) in
1979. John Hale, the chairman of Trustees, wrote to Alan
Bullock, his counterpart at the Tate, to explain the decision
to buy the Picasso

Our acquisition of the Picasso follows a pattern
established by a number of purchases made since our
negotiations towards such an arrangement started in
1975: purchases made after prior consultation, Director
to Director (as in the present case) and with no sense
that one Institution was in competition with the other
for the work in question, nor with the sense that such
purchases pre-empted the eventual settlement of a

shared overall policy of acquisition. Such purchases,
plus our knowledge that you have never seen our
concern for extending our collection in terms of such
an embargo that would be against the national interest,
provided the background to our decision.

This was not the view taken by the Trustees of the Tate, who resented the policy. But the problem of the relationship was solved, at least for a time, by a committee which met under the chairmanship of Sir Isaiah Berlin and agreed that the National Gallery should sacrifice its right to take over pictures from the Tate's collection in exchange for an acceptance that it was clearly in the National Gallery's, and the nation's, interest that the collection should extend into the twentieth century.

The problems surrounding the funding of acquisitions were partly eased by the establishment of the National Heritage Memorial Fund in 1980. This derived from the post-war Land Fund set up in 1946 by Hugh Dalton as a memorial to those who had lost their lives in the Second World War. The post-war Treasury had neglected to spend it. In 1977 the sale was announced of Mentmore, one of the great Rothschild mansions in Buckinghamshire. The National Trust was unable to acquire it, and so the house and all its contents, including 70 paintings, were sold. The National Gallery acquired one picture, *Madame de Pompadour* (NG 6440) by François-Hubert Drouais, by private treaty sale, when the whole house and its collection could have been acquired in lieu of estate duties for only £2 million. As a result of the furore surrounding the sale, a group of cross-party MPs decided that the Land Fund should be used in future to help save major houses and works of art from being sold.

Throughout the 1980s, the National Heritage Memorial Fund worked admirably as a fund of last resort to help protect the heritage, including works of art. It enabled the National Gallery to acquire Altdorfer's *Christ taking Leave of his Mother* (NG 6463) from the Wernher Collection in 1980; Claude's *Landscape with Psyche outside the Palace of Cupid* (NG 6471) in 1981 – the 'Enchanted Castle' which was so much admired by Keats and is thought to have inspired lines in his 'Ode to a Nightingale'; Poussin's *The Triumph of Pan* (NG 6477), which was owned in the nineteenth century by James Morrison, a millionaire friend of Eastlake, and was bought in 1982 from Sudeley Castle; Ter Brugghen's *The Concert* (NG 6483) in 1983; and Bassano's *The Way to Calvary* (NG 6490) in 1984. In fact, looking back at the early 1980s, it was a period of very active acquisitions, helped by the fact that, in 1984, the government provided a purchase grant of £3.3 million a year out of a total budget of just over £7 million. This made it possible for the Gallery, for example, to acquire Rubens's *Samson and Delilah* (NG 6461) from overseas straightforwardly from its own funds.

In 1985, following a reduction in the purchase grant from £3.3 million to £2.75 million, the National Gallery sought the help of individual benefactors and was rewarded by an extraordinary gift of £50 million from Paul Getty, a great philanthropist and Anglophile son of the founder of the Getty Museum, paid in two stages – £30 million in 1985 and a further £20 million two years later. This has been treated as an endowment, looked after and very shrewdly invested by the committee of the American Friends of the National Gallery, whereby the income can be used for acquisitions in order to supplement (but supposedly not replace) funding from central government.

Levey's last years as Director were somewhat clouded by the controversy over a new building on the so-called Hampton Site, which had been left vacant and used as a car park since the Second World War. In 1958, the government had acquired the site of Hampton's furniture store immediately to the west of the Wilkins Building, in the expectation that it would be used either for a new building for the National Portrait Gallery or for an extension for the National Gallery. In 1981, the Conservative government proposed that the site should be developed as a public-private partnership on behalf of the National Gallery, with galleries on the top floor and commercial office space below.

Michael Heseltine, the Secretary of State in the Department of the Environment, announced an open architectural competition for a scheme for the site in December 1981. Seven architectural practices were short-listed and their proposals were exhibited at the Gallery in late August 1982. The one favoured by the public and which, indeed, was finally selected by the Minister – against the advice of the Board of Trustees – was designed by Ahrends, Burton and Koralek. It was in a style of austere, stripped-down modernism and consisted of a circular, internal courtyard with a public right-of-way through to Leicester Square. The public's second choice was a scheme designed by Arup Associates, which at that time was led by Philip Dowson – again, quite austere and looking rather like law courts with heavily barred windows. Third choice was an extremely ambitious project proposed by Richard Rogers, which combined elements of the Pompidou Centre with external staircases which were to reappear in the Lloyds building and a high tower which looks as if it might have been designed by Dan Dare. Interestingly, it attracted both 29 per cent of the first choice votes and 36 per cent of the 'least popular'.

This competition, more than any other in Britain during the post-war period, except perhaps for the debate over Paternoster Square, was emblematic of the contest between modernists, who favoured modern solutions not necessarily related to the context of the site or the surroundings, and the post-modernists, who felt that any building on so sensitive a site should be closely related in style and fabric to its surroundings. It has perhaps been forgotten that the Gallery itself, including Michael Levey as Director and Noel Annan, his worldly chairman of Trustees, much preferred the project put forward by Skidmore, Owings and Merrill, the American architectural practice which proposed a scheme which looks rooted in the classical tradition.

# 16. NEIL MACGREGOR
## 1987–2002

In late 1985, not long after the appointment of Jacob Rothschild as chairman of Trustees, Michael Levey announced his early retirement and the job was offered to Edmund Pillsbury, a rich, young American who had been Director of the Yale Center for British Art before moving to the Kimbell Art Museum in Fort Worth. This was in spite of strong and very public objections from the staff and unions (who disapproved that such a key post in national policy should go to an American). Pillsbury turned the job down, ostensibly as a result of the controversy but as likely because it was so badly paid, and one of the Trustees, Sir Nicholas Henderson, was sent off to 10 Downing Street to persuade the Prime Minister to allow the appointment of Neil MacGregor. However accidental, it turned out to be a brilliant choice. A young Scot, brought up in Glasgow, he had been trained as a lawyer in Edinburgh before studying modern languages at Oxford and art history at the Courtauld Institute, where he was known as Anthony Blunt's favourite student. He took up the Directorship in January 1987 and brought skills of quiet, rather steely determination and a passionate Anglo-Catholic belief in the religious content of art.

Whereas Levey had spent his entire working life on the staff of the National Gallery, MacGregor came to it having been editor of the *Burlington Magazine*. His intellectual background was in the French seventeenth century and during his time as Director he was able to adjust the balance of the collection by displaying the seventeenth-century collection in the north galleries, as well as working closely with

Sir Denis Mahon, who had pledged to leave a substantial part of his extraordinary collection to the National Gallery by way of the National Art-Collections Fund (now known as the Art Fund), on condition that the National Gallery never charges an entry fee and never sells a single painting from the collection. But, in terms of acquisitions, MacGregor is perhaps best remembered for his advocacy of nineteenth-century Scandinavian and German painting and so, following Levey's example, the canon began to expand with the acquisition of Købke's *The Northern Drawbridge to the Citadel in Copenhagen* (NG 6507) in 1986, Caspar David Friedrich's *Winter Landscape* (NG 6517) in 1987 and Eduard Gaertner's *The Friedrichsgracht, Berlin* (NG 6524) in 1989.

MacGregor's arrival coincided with a whole series of changes to the way the National Gallery operated. Levey had run the Gallery as a curatorial oligarchy, whereby each of the curators took on responsibility for the running of some part of the Gallery's other affairs, including Alistair Smith who ran Education and Exhibitions, Christopher Brown who ran the Library, and Michael Wilson, who ran the Building. But this form of creative amateurism, which, following the Whitehall model, had traditionally presumed that Oxbridge graduates were the best possible people to run all aspects of the administration, was no longer felt to be desirable in a much more accountable (and Thatcherite) environment, which promoted the possession of business skills over humanistic learning. One of the Trustees, Michael Cowdy, who was bursar of King's College, Cambridge and had previously worked for the Treasury, crossed the table to become the Gallery's Head of Administration, responsible for ensuring that the gallery's private wealth was as far as possible invisible to his former colleagues. This coincided with the untying of the National Gallery from the civil service and the requirement to create a separate administrative structure, responsible for fund-raising, effective financial management, and looking after the building independently of the government's Property Services Agency, which had recently arranged the refurbishment of the Barry Rooms, but was now, probably rightly, abolished.

In retrospect, MacGregor's greatest responsibility was overseeing the installation of the Sainsbury Wing. Following the first design competition for the Hampton Site, the revised scheme by Ahrends, Burton and Koralek had been denounced by the Prince of Wales:

> Instead of designing an extension to the elegant façade
> of the National Gallery which complements it and
> continues the concept of columns and domes, it looks
> as though we may be presented with a kind of vast
> municipal fire station, complete with the sort of tower
> that contains the siren. I would understand this type
> of High Tech approach if you demolished the whole
> of Trafalgar Square and started again with a single
> architect responsible for the entire layout, but what is
> proposed is like a monstrous carbuncle on the face of a
> much loved and elegant friend.

As a result of the Prince of Wales's attack, the Trustees, with Jacob Rothschild as chairman, had gone back to the drawing board and drawn up a revised shortlist, advised by Colin Amery, the architectural critic of the *Financial Times*, and Ada Louise Huxtable, an American architectural critic. Their list consisted mostly of postmodernists or, alternatively, modernists with classical tendencies: Harry Cobb of I.M. Pei Partnership, who had been responsible for a recently opened building for the Portland Museum in Maine; Colquhoun and Miller, who had designed sensitive and reticent new galleries for the Whitechapel Art Gallery; Jeremy Dixon and BDP, who were then in the early stages of designing radical changes to the Royal Opera House, a comparably ambitious building project which involved many of the same issues of urbanism; Piers Gough of Campbell, Zogolovitch, Wilkinson and Gough, the brilliant maverick who had been responsible for the design of the Lutyens exhibition at the Hayward Gallery in 1981; James Stirling, who was then at the apogee of his international success as the designer of the new Staatsgalerie in Stuttgart, the Clore Gallery at the Tate and the Sackler Wing at the Fogg Art Museum in Cambridge, Massachusetts; and Robert Venturi of Venturi, Rauch and Scott Brown.

It is intriguing to look back at their design proposals. Cobb suggested a building whose dominant feature was a classical rotunda at the corner of the building on Trafalgar Square. John Miller suggested a form of 1930s classicism, highly rectilinear, but with a version of a Palladian window set into the façade. Jeremy Dixon proposed a hexagonal Baptistery as the entrance to the building. Piers Gough's proposal looks like a version of Edwardian baroque. James Stirling's building had Egyptian fins. The competition was won by Robert Venturi, who impressed the jury by the fact that he talked not about architecture, but about the display of the collection, and was particularly knowledgeable about Italian church interiors, having been a prize fellow at the American Academy in Rome in the mid-1950s.

The key emphasis in the Sainsbury Wing was on providing a sympathetic environment for the early Italian collection on the top floor and there can be no dispute that, in this, Robert Venturi and his wife and partner, Denise Scott Brown, succeeded brilliantly, providing a sequence of top-lit galleries, modelled on the dimensions of John Soane's Dulwich Picture Gallery. Their mood is intelligently calm, ideal for the contemplation of works of art, with a strong use of the grey Florentine sandstone known as *pietra serena*. The staircase is magnificent, but almost too monumental, a nineteenth-century idea that great works of art should be reached by climbing up into a different stratosphere. The rest of the facilities were necessarily squeezed into the site under the main floor galleries, with a restaurant looking out over Trafalgar Square and an entrance lobby, which is perhaps more reminiscent of the beaux-arts classicism of an American railway station than the crypt of an Italian church it was intended to resemble. There is a big lecture theatre downstairs and exhibition galleries in the basement, which suggest the continuing ambivalence of the National Gallery towards the benefits of temporary exhibitions, putting them as far away as possible from the permanent collection and with no access whatsoever to natural daylight.

Is the Sainsbury Wing a continuation of Wilkins or is it a deliberate contrast? The answer is a bit of both. Robert Venturi and Denise Scott Brown wanted it to be slightly more of a contrast: more open to the light and the street; less conventionally classical; playing games with the vocabulary of classical form; in fact, slightly domestic in feel, modelled on houses in the suburbs of Philadelphia. The Trustees wanted the transitions to be as seamless as possible. This modest difference in emphasis played itself out in differences of opinion as to whether or not there should be a Palladian window on the internal wall of the long gallery looking out over the restaurant onto the street, to which the Gallery objected as it would have admitted too much daylight, and whether or not there should be classical detailing, such as skirting and door surrounds, in the exhibition galleries downstairs. Most of all, there were disagreements as to whether or not there should be a free-standing Corinthian column on the front corner of the façade and a functionally redundant column in the entrance lobby.

Parallel to the debates about the design of the Sainsbury Wing was a comparable debate about the most appropriate style of display for the main galleries. By the early 1980s, there was the beginning of articulate opposition to the diversity of styles of display in the National Gallery. The young Neil MacGregor, not yet editor of the *Burlington Magazine*, had written in its December 1980 issue as follows:

> The Underground long ago overtook the weather as a source of London grousing. Both must soon be in danger of being outstripped by the **National Gallery**. The newly reopened French and Spanish rooms live sadly up to one's expectations.
>
> What are those expectations? The early Italian room was some time ago rehung without being redecorated, so that the previous hanging can still be read in dust-marks on the wall, a palimpsest of past taste. The Pieros and Botticellis have for years had to fight for attention between turquoise cornice and tangerine carpet. The seventeenth-century Italian room contrives to look like a muddled country-house saloon, where a work of the quality of Annibale's *Pietà* jostles with the third-rate.

This brief paragraph represents one of those seismic shifts in public taste away from the neutral style of gallery display, which had been very much the orthodoxy in the post-war period, towards an interest in displaying pictures as they would have been seen in the country-house galleries of the nineteenth century – a style of display first pioneered in Britain by Michael Jaffé at the Fitzwilliam in the mid-1970s, then by Timothy Clifford in his refurbishment of the Manchester City Art Gallery in the early 1980s and subsequently in the National Gallery in Edinburgh. It was part of a much wider movement towards historic revivalism, a rejection of the modernism which had been such a dominant philosophy in the arts.

Not long afterwards, an article appeared in *Private Eye*, which was presumably written by Gavin Stamp, an architectural historian who wrote articles for *Private Eye* under the pseudonym 'Piloti':

> Whatever qualifications the directors of Britain may
> have, a visual sense would not seem to be one of them.
> Compared with museums on the Continent or in the
> United States, our buildings are badly treated: the original
> architecture is not respected, nor are the alternatives of a
> quality to justify the spoiling of what is usually an historic
> and beautiful structure in its own right. All too typical is
> the National Gallery . . . which at considerable expense –
> to the taxpayer – is being continually altered and where
> the entrance hall greets the visitor like a Trust House hotel:
> lowered ceilings, stalls, desks, notice boards and hessian all
> conceal Wilkins's fine architecture.

By 1986, following the arrival of Jacob Rothschild as chairman of Trustees, there was a change of tune. Rothschild had an active interest in issues of gallery design, was sympathetic to the changes which Timothy Clifford was introducing at the National Galleries of Scotland, and was a close friend of David Mlinaric, the interior decorator who had been responsible for the refurbishment of Beningbrough Hall in Yorkshire in a style of un-archaeological, aestheticised historicism. This was the period of *The Treasure Houses of Britain* exhibition at the National Gallery of Art in Washington, when the country house was regarded as the *fons et origo* of British culture and its style of display the most appropriate environment for hanging pictures.

In November 1986 – interestingly just at the point that Neil MacGregor was appointed as Director – Stamp wrote in the *Daily Telegraph*:

Despite the lessons about the treatment of historical
interiors and the hanging of old paintings provided by
galleries throughout the world, our academic experts
have tried to treat works of art in isolation. Their ideal
has been but one painting hung on a bare, colourless
wall, ignoring the complementary power of fine
architecture and rich colour. The result has been that
so many of our museum interiors have been neutralised
with dropped ceilings, hessian walls, incongruous
display stands and gallons and gallons of white paint.

Later on in the same article, he says how

It has been the National Gallery which has triumphantly
exemplified the worst aspects of the architectural
blindness of our modern museum culture. With its
neglected and colourless galleries, tawdry innovations
and general impression of visual squalour and clutter,
the treatment of this potentially fine building has made
what should be our premier gallery into a national
scandal. Now, at long last, with Jacob Rothschild as
Chairman of the Trustees and with financial help from
J. Paul Getty junior, changes are being made – if only to
take the wind out of the sails of tiresome Mr Clifford.

This article provides the thinking behind the current
orthodoxy, known in curatorial circles as 'the heritage hang'
and described by Timothy Clifford in an article published in
the *Journal of Museum Management and Curatorship.*

But there remained differences of opinion as to how rigorously this orthodoxy should be pursued and there were
divisions behind the scenes in the late 1980s between the
aesthetes, represented by Jacob Rothschild as chairman of
Trustees and Colin Amery as his *quondam* architectural

adviser, who wanted a style of intense visual opulence, and those, including Neil MacGregor as Director, who had a slightly more didactic and democratic attitude to issues of display, who objected to David Mlinaric selecting smart, silk fabrics, not least on grounds of cost, and who regarded the style of the National Galleries of Scotland as too redolent of the elitism of the traditional picture-owning classes. They preferred the advice on issues of interior refurbishment of Purcell Miller Tritton, a well-established firm of conservation architects based in Norwich, which was employed as house architects and was responsible for working on the refurbishment of most of the galleries in the Wilkins building over the last fifteen years, including the complete reconfiguring of the north galleries, converting them from 1970s brutalism to a style which aimed to reproduce the nineteenth-century mood of the Wilkins galleries.

The characteristics of the hang during this period were that it should be as consistent as possible, lacking any modifications which might indicate the taste or interests or sensibility of an individual curator and ensuring a sense of intellectual clarity and coherence to the institution as a whole.

During the 1990s the Gallery was able to continue to make remarkable acquisitions, helped by the establishment in 1993 of the Heritage Lottery Fund and by the prudent investment of the Getty endowment. For example, in 1992, Holbein's *A Lady with a Squirrel and a Starling* (NG 6540) was acquired from Lord Cholmondeley, whose family had owned it since 1761. In 1993, Thomas Jones's cool oil sketch of *A Wall in Naples* (NG 6544) was bought from a private collection. In 1995, Bartolomé Bermejo's *Saint Michael triumphant over the Devil with the Donor Antonio Juan* (NG 6553) added a Spanish dimension as a deliberate contrast to the Gallery's collection of fifteenth-century Italian and Netherlandish paintings, while Seurat's *The Channel of Gravelines, Grand*

*Fort-Philippe* (NG 6554) was bought from Heinz Berggruen, the Paris dealer, who had previously loaned works by Van Gogh, Cézanne, Seurat, Braque and Picasso. In 1996, Dürer's *Saint Jerome* (NG 6563) was acquired from the Bacon family in Norfolk and Zurbaran's *Cup of Water and a Rose on a Silver Plate* (NG 6566) was bought from the estate of Kenneth Clark. In 1997, the Gallery was able to acquire Stubbs's great *Whistlejacket* (NG 6569) from the descendants of the second Marquess of Rockingham, who had commissioned the painting for Wentworth Woodhouse in Yorkshire.

But the great achievement of the 1990s was the inexorable rise in visitor numbers, helped by MacGregor's high public profile and success on television and by the growth of a mass democratic interest in treating art as a form of secular religion. In 1949, the number of visitors had topped a million for the first time since 1859. The next big increase was recorded in 1975, when the numbers were 2,045,847, helped no doubt by the opening of the new northern extension and by the exhibition *The Rival of Nature*. By 1985, they were over 3 million. By 1998, they were over 5 million, although it quickly became clear that numbers could not necessarily be maintained at this level once the Tate Gallery opened Tate Modern and when many other museums and galleries, including the National Portrait Gallery next door, were able to improve their facilities through grants from the National Lottery.

Half of the visitors to the National Gallery are tourists. They come to see and experience some of the greatest works of art in one of the greatest galleries in the world, equivalent in the quality and range of its collection if not in scale to the paintings collections of the Louvre, the Prado and the Uffizi. They pour in as the doors open at 10 o'clock armed with their guide books to seek out the impressionists and explore the mysteries of the history of art with quasi-religious fervour.

Half are visitors from the United Kingdom. They come sometimes only once in their lifetime as a child, but often many times throughout their lives, refreshing their consciousness by looking and feeling and reflecting on works which may be old favourites or which they have not seen before.

# ENVOI

In thinking about, and writing about, the history of the National Gallery, I have, for obvious reasons, been particularly concerned with those problems and issues that previous Directors have faced and which I was to face myself. The problems are not so very different now from what they were in the past.

The first is the relationship between the National Gallery and the state: to what extent is the National Gallery an instrument of government policy and to what extent should the Director be viewed as an appointee of the government or as a free agent with independent views or, instead, as simply subordinate to the Board of Trustees? If one visits and talks to the Directors of the Louvre or the Prado, it is quite clear that they occupy a position of considerable public authority, which is directly answerable to the government of the day. Britain has always adopted a more devolved approach, whereby the authority for the oversight of the institution is vested in the Board of Trustees, a group of people who have in the past been chosen by the Prime Minister, but normally on the advice of the chairman of the Board, but are now appointed through a process which is scrutinised by the Commissioner of Public Appointments. Members of the Board have traditionally been expected to act as guardians of the public interest. But this has never been very well defined and, in practice, they have tended to be plutocratic collectors or landowners with historic collections, and have always been inclined to want to involve themselves to a greater or lesser extent in the choice of works for the collection.

The constitutional independence of the Board of Trustees - has always produced ambiguities in the relationship with government, which has traditionally provided funding through the public purse, although since the 1980s this has been expected to be supplemented by the profits of commercial enterprise. Does the money from government come with strings attached? In practice, it is clear that the National Gallery has worked best where there is not too much friction between the Trustees and parliament. In the nineteenth century, acquisitions and their quality were a matter of often passionate debate in the House of Commons and it is impressive how, during the 1830s, 1840s and early 1850s, the operation of the National Gallery was so frequently discussed and that it should have been the subject of so many Select Committees to investigate its responsibilities and activities.

One would not necessarily wish to return to this state of affairs, but it was symptomatic of the fact that the government of the day often recognised that the National Gallery, how it operates, who it serves and what its status is in terms of public education, are matters of public interest. It is arguable that the period where there was most determined effort to grapple with the problems of funding for acquisitions was in the early 1920s when Sir Philip Sassoon, a recent government minister, was able directly to influence government thinking. I found it mildly depressing during my time as Director how relatively little the government is now interested in the National Gallery, how immune to the siren calls for the funding of acquisitions, but this is probably because its current allegiance is to Tate Modern as an emblem of cultural modernisation, as well as the fact that the gradual professionalisation of political life means that far fewer MPs have any well-developed interest in the national collections.

The second issue which engaged me is the nature of the relationship between the Board of Trustees and the Director.

In looking back over the National Gallery's history, it is evident that this has too frequently been a source of tension, perhaps deriving from a cultural memory of the early days when it was unequivocally run by the Trustees and the Keeper was merely an agent of what they wanted done. In 1855, this position was rectified by a proper constitution which vested full authority in Charles Eastlake as Director, while the Board of Trustees was restricted to the role of representing the National Gallery to the government and the public. But, in the course of the late nineteenth century, this restriction was clearly regarded as frustrating by the Trustees, who resented the autonomy over acquisitions allowed to Sir Frederic Burton and who therefore ensured that Sir Edward Poynter was appointed following the terms of the so-called Rosebery Minute. Poynter hated the amount of interference which the Trustees had over his policy of acquisitions, as did Sir Charles Holroyd, who was treated atrociously. Sir Charles Holmes, on the other hand, was able to play the Treasury off against his Trustees. Kenneth Clark got on well with his Trustees, but was accordingly detested by his staff.

It is arguable that this relationship has improved in the post-war period and it is certainly true that Philip Hendy had a good relationship with Lionel Robbins, the economist at the London School of Economics who helped resolve the dispute when the Trustees wanted to terminate his appointment and who subsequently served three terms as chairman, and, likewise, by all accounts, Michael Levey had a good relationship with John Hale. This was the period described by Noel Annan, who succeeded Hale as chairman, in his book *Our Age*, which describes the post-war liberal consensus which respected intellectual and academic authority. But this consensus, regarded as too cosy by Margaret Thatcher, who wished to restore the rule of the rich, was overturned during the 1980s and I am not persuaded that the relationship between

Neil MacGregor and his Trustees was always straightforward and it was certainly not during my time as Director. There is something in the character of the National Gallery, perhaps its centrality and prestige in national culture, which has historically led to this tension, most probably a combination of the fact that the National Gallery has always had monthly meetings of the Board of Trustees, which has inevitably led to a great deal of interference in matters of administrative detail, and because appointment to the Board of Trustees has frequently gone to people who are powerful in other spheres of public life and who therefore expect to exert the same amount of autocratic control as elsewhere.

The third issue which interested me is the changing shape of the collection. It is currently assumed that the National Gallery is an institution devoted solely to the study and display of Old Master paintings and that this has always been so. But it is not actually true. When the National Gallery was founded, part of its founding idea was that it should display Old Master paintings alongside modern British work in order to enable comparison between the two and the Royal Academy was located next door to the National Gallery in order to ensure a healthy exchange between examples of works of art from the past and the practice of art in the present. In 1876, when the Barry Rooms opened, the majority of the galleries in the Wilkins building were devoted to British painting. When Charles Holmes went off to Paris to bid for paintings at the Degas sale in the closing weeks of the First World War, his view as to what he might acquire was not restricted solely to the nineteenth-century French paintings which Degas had owned, but it was certainly open to him to acquire works by Degas himself and his younger contemporaries. In the post-war period, different views as to the appropriate character and shape of the collection and where its boundary should be with modern and contemporary art have been evident in the recurrent tensions in the relationship between the National Gallery and the Tate, beginning with the Tate Act in 1955 which gave the National Gallery freedom to take over works of art from the Tate, once they were regarded as appropriate to join the canon of greatness represented by the collection of the National Gallery.

There have been several occasions in the past when Directors have sought to expand the boundaries of the collection, as when Sir Frederic Burton bought a series of Graeco-Roman mummy portraits in 1888, now transferred to the British Museum, and Charles Holmes tried to buy a collection of Persian paintings in 1924, an icon in 1926, and Chinese frescoes in 1927. This is clearly an issue which is likely to preoccupy future Directors as to whether or not the National Gallery can afford to remain a fortress of western European painting only, devoted to the study and interpretation of a geography of art which may appear increasingly anachronistic, or whether or not it should begin to collect, for example, nineteenth-century American paintings or Russian. And I was of the view, as was Sir Michael Levey, that it should not retain a strict boundary of 1900, which appears increasingly old-fashioned – a residue of the hostility towards modernism in the early twentieth century and ignoring the fact that there are great, classic paintings of the twentieth century which would benefit from being seen alongside those of the past.

The fourth issue which preoccupied, and sometimes frustrated, me is the issue as to how to afford increasingly expensive acquisitions. I viewed the National Gallery as an organic entity, continually growing, shaped by changing intellectual interests and the tastes of its Directors and staff, like a slow moving stream, which is enhanced, generation by generation, and never static. In writing this book, it is possible to discern different generations of taste, beginning with the country-house connoisseurs of the 1820s, through the more saccharine, religious taste of the high Victorians, to a preoccupation with works of art in British private collections and an interest in Spanish painting in the 1880s and 1890s. In the twentieth century, the shape and character of the collection has continued to change, beginning with the acquisition of a remarkable group of Impressionists funded by Samuel Courtauld and including a deliberate state-funded effort to acquire more nineteenth-century French painting during the 1950s, as well as a shift in emphasis in the 1990s back towards the Baroque.

But during my first week as Director in July 2002, Rubens's *Massacre of the Innocents* sold for £49.5 million. Not long afterwards, the National Gallery was informed that Raphael's *Madonna of the Pinks* had been sold to the Getty Museum for £35 million. The price of Old Master paintings is now prodigious. And the means of the National Gallery to acquire them is relatively restricted, in spite of the availability of considerable private trust funds, guarded by independent Trustees, on both sides of the Atlantic. It has become clear that the traditional way of acquiring works of art by going out into the international market place is increasingly problematic. New solutions will have to be found through changing the tax system, by encouraging life-time gifts of works of art from individuals or, as on the continent, gifts of works of art from corporations through generous tax deductions (in Spain as much as 100 per cent), if the collections of the National Gallery are to continue to grow as they have in the past.

The fifth issue which has been a theme throughout this book is perhaps a more personal one in that I have long been interested in the ways in which the buildings of the National Gallery have shaped the experience of looking at paintings. Some people think that all you have to do with paintings is to put them on the wall in order to enjoy them. But it should be obvious that the way that pictures are hung, their relationship one to another, the way that they are lit, the ways in which they are ordered, profoundly alters how they are perceived. In the early nineteenth century, they were hung without labels or documentation apart from the names of the artist on the frame, because it was presumed that gentlemen of taste would know who the pictures were by. All that was required was a handlist.

In the later nineteenth century, pictures were hung by national schools, which was viewed as the key way by which to classify them and visitors were provided with catalogues. When Kenneth Clark became Director, he hung the pictures by eye as a man of taste. Philip Hendy was a modernist, liking a style of display which kept the pictures at a great distance from one another, following the model of American museums. Since the 1980s, the fashion has been for what is known as a 'heritage hang', simulating the appearance of the princely interiors in which works of art were originally displayed, although this has never included double hanging, while the Sainsbury Wing was designed to replicate the more contemplative atmosphere of a Renaissance church.

Finally, I cannot disguise or dispute the fact that, during the course of writing this book, I became increasingly interested in exploring a fault-line which seems to run throughout the history of the National Gallery.

On the one hand, there is no doubt that there were, and are, many people involved in the affairs of the National Gallery who have been motivated by a clear sense of public idealism, of wanting to convert what traditionally was a private interest in Old Master paintings into a public benefit. In his early sixties, Charles Eastlake embarked on an intelligent campaign to create a collection on profoundly historical principles and succeeded in building the collection in a short space of time from being rather amateurish to being one of the greatest collections in Europe. During the 1920s, Charles

Holmes, who is one of the Directors whose achievements have been least recognised, realised the importance of acquiring modern paintings with modest resources and understood the importance of the National Gallery as a vehicle of public education. Kenneth Clark intuitively understood the ways in which the National Gallery could be a source of inspiration and consolation to the general public throughout the Second World War and, through the displays of the Picture of the Month, encouraged the contemplation of individual works of art. Michael Levey had a strong belief in the ideal of bringing an understanding of art to children and wrote beautifully about works of art, particularly of the eighteenth century. And my predecessor, Neil MacGregor, has been a great source of public inspiration in revitalising an interest in the religious content of art.

And yet, as one studies the history of the National Gallery, it is an inescapable fact that there has been a countervailing tendency that has led to nearly continuous tension between the Directors and their Trustees. In its early days, the National Gallery was run by a small coterie of the political and social elite, members of the cabinet and prominent collectors and politicians. In the later nineteenth century, the political elite was replaced by members of the landed aristocracy and hereditary peerage alongside ultra-rich collectors. In the late nineteenth and early twentieth century, there was too often a tendency for the Trustees to treat their Directors, as Alfred de Rothschild described it, as they would their butlers. Sir Edward Poynter was so disgusted by the lack of respect shown for his experience and expertise that he did not seek reappointment. Charles Holroyd was also treated badly and was driven to an early grave. Charles Holmes took a form of revenge on his Trustees when he came to write his autobiography. Sir Augustus Daniel resigned from the post of Director even in spite of himself having been a Trustee.

Looking back at the history of the National Gallery from the vantage point of the twenty-first century, it is a curious narrative. Born out of eighteenth-century indifference to the public subsidy of art institutions, dogged by frequent stinginess on the part of the state, it has been made possible, most of all, by a small number of outstandingly generous connoisseurs and donors, who have had a sense of public duty and of the opportunity that is afforded by the study and enjoyment of great works of art; but also by the occasional interventions of politicians, and even Prime Ministers, who have had an understanding that politics can, and should, extend beyond the realm of bread and circuses into the belief that each generation should seize the opportunity to acquire works of art as they become available on the market (or are offered by private owners) in order to add masterpieces to the national collection.

Charles Eastlake emerges as the greatest hero of the story, initially resigning from the office of Keeper and subsequently returning as Director, able to buy works of art adventurously in Italy at a time when they were relatively freely available and to put the Gallery and its operation on a sound administrative footing. It was Eastlake who ensured that Britain possesses a National Gallery which may not equal the princely magnificence of the Louvre or the Prado or the Kunsthistorisches Museum in Vienna, but has its own range and integrity as a relatively small-scale public collection of extraordinarily consistent high quality, which has grown slightly haphazardly and pragmatically through the actions of a small group of devoted public servants. I salute my predecessors, who have grappled with so many of the same problems as I did, frequently with greater success, and I wish my successor well in the task which lies before him.

# BIBLIOGRAPHY

## Origins

The first attempt to write a history of the National Gallery appeared in the centenary volume by Charles Holmes and C.H. Collins Baker, *The Making of the National Gallery: An Historical Sketch*, London, 1924. Michael Levey wrote a Pitkin Pictorial under the title *A Brief History of the National Gallery*, first published in 1957, and Philip Hendy published *The National Gallery*, London, 1960. In 1974 (the Gallery's 150th anniversary), Gregory Martin, then an Assistant Keeper, published nine articles on 'The Founding of the National Gallery' in *Connoisseur* and Cecil Gould, the Gallery's Keeper, produced *Failure and Success: 150 Years of the National Gallery 1824–74*, London, 1974. More recently, there has been a considerable amount of analysis of the early history, including 'From the Princely Gallery to the Public Art Museum: the Louvre Museum and the National Gallery, London' in Carol Duncan, *Civilizing Rituals: Inside Public Art Museums*, London, 1995, pp. 21–47, Brandon Taylor, 'The Paths to the National Gallery', *Art for the Nation: Exhibitions and the London public 1747–2001*, Manchester, 1999, pp.29–66, Colin Trodd, 'The paths to the National Gallery' in Paul Barlow and Colin Trodd (eds.), *Governing Cultures: Art Institutions in Victorian London*, Aldershot, 2000, pp.30–43 and Holger Hoock, 'Old Masters and the English School: the Royal Academy of Arts and the notion of a national gallery at the turn of the nineteenth century', *Journal of the History of Collections*, 16:1, 2004, pp.1–18. See, also, Giles Waterfield, 'The Development of the Early Art Museum in Britain' in P. Bjurström (ed.), *The Genesis of the Art Museum in the 18th*

Century, Stockholm, 1993, pp.81–111 and Jonathan Conlin, 'The Origins and History of the National Gallery, 1753–1860', unpublished Ph.D. Thesis, Cambridge University, 2002.

## William Seguier

William Seguier is the subject of Alastair Laing, 'William Seguier and Advice to Picture Collectors' in Christine Sitwell and Sarah Staniforth (eds.), *Studies in the History of Painting Restoration*, London, 1998, pp.97–120 and of a long article in Judy Egerton, *National Gallery Catalogues: The British School*, pp.388–98. John Julius Angerstein is the subject of Anthony Twist, *John Julius Angerstein, 1735–1823*, Lewiston NY, 2006. George Beaumont and his collection are studied in Felicity Owen and David Blayney Brown, *Collector of Genius: A Life of Sir George Beaumont*, New Haven and London, 1988 and there is a great deal of information about early collectors in Thomas Tuohy, *A Taste for Pictures: The Formation and Dispersal of British Private Collections, 1630–1930*, London, 2009. On the early history of the building, there is Gregory Martin, 'Wilkins and the National Gallery', *Burlington Magazine*, June 1971, pp.318–29, Rhodri Liscombe, *William Wilkins 1778–1839*, Cambridge, 1980, the relevant section of J. Mordaunt Crook and M.H. Port (eds.), *The History of the King's Works*, vol. VI, 1782–1851, London, 1973, pp.461–70, and David Watkin and Rhodri Liscombe, *The Age of Wilkins*, Cambridge, 2000. I have published a version of chapter II under the title 'The design and construction of the National Gallery' in Frank Salmon (ed.), *The Persistence of the Classical: Essays on Architecture Presented to David Watkin*, London, 2008, pp.124–35.

## Thomas Uwins

The life of Thomas Uwins is recorded in Sarah Uwins, *A Memoir of Thomas Uwins*, 2 vols., London, 1858. For the work of Pennethorne, see Geoffrey Tyack, '"A gallery worthy of the British people": James Pennethorne's designs for the National Gallery, 1845–1867', *Architectural History*, vol. 33, 1990, pp.120–34 and Geoffrey Tyack, *James Pennethorne and the Making of Victorian London*, Cambridge, 1992. There is a good account of the change in taste from classical to pre-Raphaelite in Jenny Graham, *Inventing Van Eyck: The Remaking of an Artist for the Modern Age*, Oxford, 2007.

### Sir Charles Eastlake

There is a full biography of Charles Eastlake in David Robertson, *Sir Charles Eastlake and the Victorian art world*, Princeton, 1978 and a more recent study in Christopher Hodkinson, 'In the National Interest: Sir Charles Eastlake and the National Gallery's collection of Italian Renaissance Paintings', unpublished MA dissertation, Lancaster University, 2004. The cleaning controversy of 1846 is the subject of Norman Bromelle, 'Controversy in 1846 over the Cleaning of Pictures in the National Gallery', *Museums Journal*, February 1957, pp.257–62, Jaynie Anderson, 'The First Cleaning Controversy at the National Gallery, 1846–1853' in *Appearance, Opinion, Change: Evaluating the Look of Paintings*, London, 1990, pp.3–7, and Sheldon Keck, 'Some Picture Cleaning Controversies: Past and Present', *Journal of the American Institute for Conservation*, 23, no.2, Spring 1984, pp.73–87 and there is additional information about issues of conservation in Hero Boothroyd Brooks, 'Practical developments in English Easel-Painting Conservation, c.1828–1968, from written sources', Ph.D thesis, University of London, 1999. There is an article about Otto Mündler in Tancred Borenius, 'Eastlake's Travelling Agent for the National Gallery', *Burlington Magazine*, LXXXIII, 1943, pp. 211–16 and his journals have been edited by Jaynie Anderson, 'Otto Mündler and his Travel Diary', *Walpole Society*, 51, 1985.

Information about issues of provenance appears in the relevant National Gallery catalogues, particularly in the Appendix of Collectors' Biographies in Nicholas Penny, *The Sixteenth Century Italian Paintings*, vol. 1, *Paintings from Bergamo, Brescia and Cremona*, London, 2004, pp.354–96 and vol.2, *Venice 1540–1600*, London, 2008, pp.443–74, and in Susanna Avery-Quash, 'The Growth of Interest in Early Italian Painting in Britain with particular reference to pictures in the National Gallery' in Dillian Gordon, *National Gallery Catalogues: The Fifteenth Century Italian Paintings*, vol.1, London, 2003, pp.xxiv–xliv. The most comprehensive study of the National Gallery from 1850 to 1874 appears in Christopher Whitehead, *The Public Art Museum in Nineteenth Century Britain: The Development of the National Gallery*, Aldershot, 2005, which can be supplemented by Charlotte Klonk, 'Mounting Vision: Charles Eastlake and the National Gallery of London', *Art Bulletin*, LXXXII, no.2, June 2000, pp.331–47.

### Sir William Boxall

The only studies of Boxall are Michael Liversidge, 'John Ruskin and William Boxall', *Apollo*, LXXXV, 1967, pp. 39–44 and Michael Levey, 'A Little-known Director: Sir William Boxall', *Apollo*, CI, 1975, pp. 354–359. The architecture of the Barry Rooms is the subject of Christopher Whitehead, 'Architectures of Display at the National Gallery: the Barry Rooms as art historiography and the problems of reconstructing historical gallery space', *Journal of the History of Collections*, 17:2, 2005, pp.189–211.

### Sir Frederic Burton

Sir Frederic Burton is the subject of Homan Potterton, 'A Director with Discrimination', *Country Life*, CLV, 9 May 1974, pp.1140–41. The work of the John Dibblee Crace is covered by Megan Aldrich (ed.), *The Craces: Royal Decorators 1768–1899*, Brighton 1990.

### Sir Edward Poynter

There is much information about Poynter's work as an artist, but little about his period of office as Director. He appears in the background of Judith Flanders, *A Circle of Sisters: Alice Kipling, Georgiana Burne-Jones, Agnes Poynter and Louisa Baldwin*, London, 2001. Andrea Geddes Poole has studied the workings of Board of Trustees at the time in 'Conspicuous Presumption: The National Gallery of Great Britain's Board of Trustees and the Decline of Aristocratic Cultural Authority 1890–1939', unpublished Ph.D. thesis, University of Toronto, 1995. A summary account appears in Andrea Geddes Poole, 'Conspicuous Presumption: The Treasury and the Trustees of the National Gallery, 1890–1939', *Twentieth-Century History*, 16:1, 2005, pp. 1–28, and she has developed its thesis in *Stewards of Culture: Contested Cultural Authority 1890–1934*, Manchester, 2009. The foundation of the National Art-Collections Fund is covered by Mary Lago, *Christina Herringham and the Edwardian Art World*, London, 1996.

### Sir Charles Holroyd

For attitudes to cultural property at the turn of the century, including a chapter on Holbein's *Christina of Denmark*, see Jordanna Bailkin, *The Culture of Property: The Crisis of Liberalism in Modern Britain*, Chicago, 2004, which should be read in conjunction with Henry James, *The Outcry*, of which there are recent editions from Penguin and the New York Review of Books. For the Mond Bequest, see Charles Saumarez Smith and Giorgia Mancini, *Ludwig Mond's Bequest: A Gift to the Nation*, London, 2006.

## Sir Charles Holmes

Charles Holmes wrote an entertaining and sardonic auto-biography, *Self and Partners – Mostly Self. Being the reminiscences of C.J. Holmes*, London, 1936. His trip to Paris with Maynard Keynes is described in Quentin Bell, 'A Cézanne in the Hedge' in Hugh Lee (ed.), *A Cézanne in the Hedge and other memories of Charleston and Bloomsbury*, London, 1992, pp.136–9. For Samuel Courtauld's interest in impressionism, see John House (ed.), *Impressionism for England: Samuel Courtauld as Patron and Collector*, London, 1994.

## Sir Kenneth Clark

Kenneth Clark described his time as Director of the National Gallery in *Another part of the Wood: A Self-portrait*, London, 1974, pp.211–78. He is also the subject of racy biography by Meryle Secrest, *Kenneth Clark: A Biography*, London, 1984, written shortly before his death. See, also, David Cannadine, *Kenneth Clark: From National Gallery to National Icon*, London, 2002. Sir Michael Levey wrote Clark's obituary, 'Kenneth Mackenzie Clark 1903–1983', *Proceedings of the British Academy*, LXX, 1984, p.394. For information about the National Gallery during the second world war, see Neil MacGregor, *'To the Happier Carpenter': Rembrandt's War-Heroine Margaretha de Geer,the London Public and the Right to Pictures*, Groningen, 1995, N.J. McCamley, *Saving Britain's Art Treasures*, Barnsley, 2003 and Suzanne Bosman, *The National Gallery in Wartime*, London, 2008. For a discussion of Clark's hanging policies, and those of subsequent Directors, see Charles Saumarez Smith, 'Narratives of Display at the National Gallery, London', *Art History*, 30:4, September 2007, pp.611–27.

## Sir Philip Hendy

There is extremely little published on the post-war history of the National Gallery, other than the unpublished autobiography by Cecil Gould, 'Tosca's Creed: Autobiography of an Art Historian', the manuscript of which is held by the National Gallery's archive. Jonathan Conlin's book, *The Nation's Mantelpiece: A History of the National Gallery*, London, 2006, includes good material on this period, but, otherwise, one has to rely on information from annual reports and folk memory.

## Sir Martin Davies

The National Gallery published a commemorative booklet on Martin Davies following his death in 1975 and there are obituaries by Michael Levey, 'Sir Martin Davies', *Burlington Magazine*, 117, 1975, pp.729–31 and Ellis Waterhouse, 'Martin Davies, 1908–1975', *Proceedings of the British Academy*, 61, 1975, pp.561–5, as well as an entry in the *Dictionary of National Biography* by Gregory Martin.

## Sir Michael Levey

Michael Levey's period as Director is probably the least well documented. He wrote an autobiography of his early life, *The Chapel is on Fire*, London, 2000, but it stops just at the moment he was appointed to the staff of the National Gallery and although he wrote illuminating accounts of, for example, Ellis Waterhouse and Martin Davies for the *Burlington Magazine*, he never published a record of his long service at the National Gallery.

## Neil MacGregor

On the Sainsbury Wing, see Colin Amery, *A Celebration of Art and Architecture: The National Gallery Sainsbury Wing*, London, 1991 and the extensive press coverage at the time that it opened, including a special issue of the *Architect's Journal*, 194: 7, August 1991 and an interview with Robert Venturi in *Post-Modern Triumphs in London*, ed. Charles Jencks, London, 1991. The work of Venturi and his partner, Denise Scott Brown, has been the subject of much recent examination, including Stanislaus von Moos, *Venturi, Scott Brown and Associates*, New York, 1999, and an exhibition catalogue, *Out of the Ordinary: Robert Venturi, Denise Scott Brown and Associates*, Philadelphia, 2001. Attitudes to display are studied by Timothy Clifford, 'The Historical Approach to the Display of Paintings', *The International Journal of Museum Management and Curatorship*, 1:2, June 1982, 93–106 and Emma Barker and Annabel Thomas, 'The Sainsbury Wing and beyond: the National Gallery today' in Emma Barker (ed.), *Contemporary Cultures of Display*, New Haven and London, 1999, 73–101. On recent building developments, see Charles Saumarez Smith 'Making an Entrance at the National Gallery', *Apollo*, September 2005, pp.24–9 and Kenneth Powell, *The National Gallery, London*, London, 2006.

# ACKNOWLEDGEMENTS

In writing this history, I was deeply indebted for a great deal of help and advice to Jonathan Conlin, who allowed me to read the chapters of his own much more authoritative history, now published under the title *The Nation's Mantelpiece: A History of the National Gallery*, as they were written, and to many former colleagues in the National Gallery, particularly the staff of my office, Anne Luckhurst and Eleanor Richards, and the archivist, Alan Crookham. I am also especially grateful to those who allowed me to consult, and learn from, their dissertations, including Christopher Whitehead, Christopher Hodkinson and Andrea Geddes Poole. The first chapter on 'Origins' is based on the annual Robertson Lecture given at the Holburne Museum in Bath in November 2005. The chapters which include information on the history of the building are based on a lecture given to the Victorian Society in October 2005 and on the annual Robert Adam lecture at Avington Park, repeated at the RIBA. Material on attitudes to display derives from a conference paper on 'Narratives of display at the National Gallery' delivered at the University of Nottingham in January 2007, which included information supplied by Fram Dinshaw and Sir Michael Levey. I was also helped by audiences of lectures I gave at the Courtauld Institute, the Whitworth Art Gallery and the University of St Andrews. Since the text was first written, a number of friends read either parts of or the full draft text and greatly improved it by their comments, criticisms and corrections. They include Tim Barringer, Christopher Brown, David Cannadine, Fintan Cullen, David Ekserdjian, James Fenton, Ivan Gaskell, Francis Russell, Jenny Uglow, Amanda Vickery and Felicity Woolf. Caroline Elam, my former Director of

Studies at Cambridge, provided very detailed suggestions on nearly every page of the text, as did Jonathan Conlin and Nicholas Penny. I owe the arrangements for publication to my brother John, who suggested John Nicoll as publisher, and to Maggie Hanbury, my long-standing and loyal literary agent. Nicholas Penny and the Board of Trustees agreed to the transfer of copyright. At a late stage, Marc Pachter, a friend and former Director of the National Portrait Gallery in Washington, made very helpful suggestions as to how the text could be improved. Douglas Matthews has done the index.

I should end by recording my debt of gratitude to the Board of Trustees for appointing me, to those trustees who sustained me by their friendship, and to my family, Romilly, Otto and Ferdinand, to whom this book is dedicated.

# INDEX

Aberdeen, George Hamilton-Gordon, 4th Earl of, 32, 39, 44, 66
Aberystwyth: National Library of Wales, 128
Adelaide, Queen of William IV, 38
Aders, Carl, 39
Agar Ellis, George *see* Dover, 1st Baron
Agnew's (art dealers), 102
Ahrends, Burton and Koralek (architects), 151, 155
Albert, Prince Consort, 65–6, 76
Altdorfer, Albrecht: *Christ taking Leave of his Mother*, 150
American Friends of the National Gallery, 150
Amery, Colin, 155, 160
Angelico, Fra: *Assumption of the Virgin*, 98; *Christ glorified in the Court of Heaven*, 79; *Dormition*, 98
Angerstein, John Julius: portrait, 7; art collection, 18–19, 33–4, 37; death, 21; paintings purchased for NG, 22–3, 25, 33–4; house purchased and occupied by NG, 25–7, 39, 42, 51; proposed demolition of house, 41
Angerstein, John (John Julius's son), 22
Annan, Noel, Baron, 152, 166; *Our Age* (book), 166
Annenberg, Walter, 145
Anrep, Helen, 124
Antwerp, 13
Aretino, Spinello: *Two Haloed Mourners*, 71
Art Fund (*earlier* National Art-Collections Fund): established, 99; appeals for Velázquez's *Rokeby Venus*, 102–3; and Holbein's *Christina of Denmark*, 106; supports purchase of Titian's *Vendramin Family*, 120; and Leonardo Cartoon, 141; and Mahon collection, 154
*Art Journal*, 77
*Art Union*, 59
art works: export, 105–8, 144
Arundel, Thomas Howard, Earl of: Rubens portrait of, 98, 108
Arup Associates, 151
Ashburnham Collection, 98
Athenaeum Club, London, 29, 40
*Athenaeum, The* (journal), 56
Augustus II (the Strong), King of Poland, 12

Bacon family (of Norfolk), 162
Baker, Charles Collins, 8, 117, 120–1; *Lely*

*and the Stuart Portrait Painters*, 120
Baldovinetti, Alesso: *Portrait of a Lady in Yellow*, 81
Baldwin, Stanley (*later* 1st Earl), 119
Balniel, David Alexander Robert Lindsay, Lord *see* Crawford, 27th Earl of
Bangor: Prichard-Jones Hall, University College, 128
Banks, Robert Richardson, 78
Banks, Thomas, 95
Baring, Alexander, 21, 24
Barker, Alexander, 79, 86
Barry, Sir Charles, 46, 55, 63
Barry, Charles, junior, 78
Barry, Edward Middleton, 84, 87–8, 94
Barry, James, 14
Bartolommeo, Fra: *The Virgin adoring the Child with St Joseph*, 105
Bassano, Jacopo da: *The Way to Calvary*, 150
Bath, John Alexander Thynne, 4th Marquess of, 92
BDP (architects), 155
Beaucousin, Edmond, 75
Beaumont, Sir George, 18–23, 27–9, 31–5, 37
Beckford, William, 52, 56, 89
Bell, Clive, 115
Bell, Vanessa, 114–15
Bellini, Giovanni, 105; *Doge Leonardo Loredan*, 56; *Virgin and Child* (*Madonna of the Pomegranate*), 71
Belvedere Gallery, Vienna, 12
Benson, Robert (known as Robin), 117
Berenson, Bernard, 98, 123
Berggruen, Heinz, 162
Berlin: Altes Museum, 50–1; Kaiser Friedrich Museum, 88, 98; Royal Gallery, 52
Berlin, Sir Isaiah, 149
Bermejo, Bartolomé: *Saint Michael triumphant over the Devil with the Donor Antonio Juan*, 161
Betjeman, (Sir) John, 130
Bianconi collection, Bologna, 70
Blaenau Ffestiniog *see* Manod Quarry
Blenheim Palace: art collection, 90
Bode, Wilhelm, 88, 98
Bosch, Hieronymus: *Christ Mocked (The Crowning with Thorns)*, 127
Boston: Museum of Fine Arts, 98
Botticelli, Sandro: *Venus and Mars*, 86;

# Index

Botticelli (*cont.*): *Virgin and Child, St John and the Angel* (tondo), 70; *Virgin and Child, St John and Two Angels* (tondo; attrib.), 69

Botticini, Francesco: *Assumption of the Virgin*, 89

Bourgeois, Sir Francis, 17

Bouts, Dirk: *Portrait of a Man*, 87

Boxall, Sir William: appointed Director (1865), 81; travels abroad, 81–2; acquisitions, 82, 85; and rebuilding of NG, 83–4; succeeded by Burton, 86

Boydell, John: Shakespeare Gallery (London), 16

Boys, Thomas Shotter, 95

Bradford, Selina, Countess of, 86

Bridgewater, Francis Egerton, 3rd Duke of, 14

Britain: and retention of art works, 13; country house sales, 89; and export of art works, 105–8, 144

British Institution: founded, 16–18, 28; offers funds for development of Pall Mall site, 41; proposed amalgamation of art and architecture department with NG, 76

British Museum: Desenfans proposes giving collection to, 15–17; suggested for gallery of paintings, 20–1, 24–5

*British Painting since Whistler* exhibition (1940), 129

British School: accommodated in NG, 88, 93

Britton, John, 19

Bromley, R.N., 110

Bronzino (Angelo di Cosimo di Mariano): *Allegory of Venus and Cupid*, 75–6; *Portrait of a Lady*, 97

Brown, Christopher, 154

Browse, Lillian, 129–30

Buccleuch, John Charles Montagu-Douglas-Scott, 7th Duke of, 127

Buchanan, William, 34

*Builder, The* (periodical), 88, 92

Bullock, Alan, Baron, 148

Bunsen, Baron Christian Carl Josias, 52

Burlington House: as proposed location for NG, 77–8; Italian Art exhibition (1930), 123

*Burlington Magazine*, 101, 107, 114, 121, 126, 153

Burne-Jones, Sir Edward, 96

Burton, Sir Frederic: appointed Director (1874), 86; acquisitions, 86–7, 166, 168; and purchase of Marlborough paintings, 90; retirement, 94–5; style, 94; accused of over-independence, 97

Butler, Samuel, 109

Byron, George Gordon, 6th Baron, 71

Calder, Alexander, 133

Campbell, Zogolovitch, Wilkinson and Gough (architects), 156

Campin, Robert, 75; *Virgin and Child before a Fire Screen*, 105

Canaletto (Giovanni Antonio Canal): *The Stonemason's Yard*, 34

Cannadine, David, 8

Cappelle, Jan van de, 87

Carlisle, Frederick Howard, 5th Earl of, 15

Carlisle, George James Howard, 9th Earl of, 98, 99, 107

Carlisle, Rosalind, Countess of, 107

Carlton House, Pall Mall, 43–4, 46, 48

Carlyle, Thomas, 86

Carracci, Annibale: *Christ appearing to St Peter on the Appian Way*, 36; *Pietà*, 158; *Three Maries*, 108

Castle Howard, Yorkshire, 15, 98, 107–8

Cennini, Cennino: *Il libro dell'arte*, 99

Cézanne, Paul, 115–16, 124, 127; *Bathers*, 142; *An Old Woman with a Rosary*, 140

Chantrey Bequest, 108

Chardin, Jean Siméon: *The House of Cards*, 116; *Young Schoolmistress*, 116

Charles I, King, 63, 91, 119

Charles, Prince of Wales, 155

Cholmondeley, David George Philip Cholmondeley, 7th Marquess of, 161

Churchill, (Sir) Winston, 119, 128

Cima da Conegliano: *S. Jerome in a Landscape*, 89

Civil Contingencies Fund, 141

Clark, Sir Kenneth (*later* Baron): wealth, 7, 123; succeeds Daniel as Director, 119, 123; background and career, 123; rehangs collection, 124–5, 170; appoints staff and assistants, 126; favours cleaning of pictures, 126–7; acquisitions, 127–8; unpopularity with staff, 128, 132, 166; and wartime evacuation of pictures, 128; on audiences at wartime concerts, 129; chairs War Artist's Advisory Committee, 130; resigns, 132; and Calouste Gulbenkian collection, 137; discovers stored Turner sketches, 139; art collection, 162; relations with Trustees, 166; and role of NG in Second World War, 171; *Another Part of the Wood* (autobiography), 123

Clarke, Francis: bequest, 89

Claude Lorrain: influence on British painters, 37; hanging, 53, 73; *Landscape with Cephalus and Procris*, 33; *Landscape with David at the Cave of Adullam*, 37; *Landscape with a Goatherd and Goat*, 34; *Landscape with Hagar and the Angel*, 34; *Landscape with the Marriage of Isaac and Rebecca*, 33; *Landscape with Narcissus and Echo*, 34; *Landscape with Psyche outside the Palace of Cupid* ('the Enchanted Castle'), 150; *A Seaport*, 33; *Seaport with the Embarkation of the Queen of Sheba*, 33; *Seaport with the Embarkation of Saint Ursula*, 34

# Index

Clifford, Timothy, 158–60
'Clique, The' (group of artists), 31
Cobb, Harry, 155–6
Cockerell, Charles Robert, 43–4, 55
Cockerell, Sir Sydney Carlyle, 113
Colborne, Ridley, 21, 43
Cole, Sir Henry, 82; *Felix Summerly's Hand-Book for the National Gallery*, 54
Coleorton Hall, Leicestershire, 35
Coleridge, Samuel Taylor, 39
Colnaghi's (art dealers), 105
Colquhoun and Miller (architects), 155
Colvin, Sir Sidney, 95
Committee of Taste, 18
Commons, House of: votes moneys to NG, 36, 77; supports purchase of Marlborough paintings, 91; debates affairs at NG, 165
Coningham, William, 62; *Picture Cleaning in the National Gallery with some Observations on the Royal Academy*, 59
Conlin, Jonathan, 8; *The Nation's Mantelpiece: A History of the National Gallery*, 9
Constable, John: opposes founding of NG, 23; admires Claude, 34; reputation, 139
Constable, W.G., 121
Coremans, Paul, 137
Correggio, Antonio Allegri da: *Christ taking leave of his Mother*, 117; *Ecce Homo*, 38; *Madonna of the basket*, 35; *Mercury instructing Cupid before Venus*, 53; *Venus with Mercury and Cupid*, 38
Cotes, Charles, 93
Courbet, Gustave: *Still Life with Apples and a Pomegranate*, 140
Courtauld Institute: founded, 120–1
Courtauld, Samuel, 116, 120, 169
Cowdy, Michael, 154
Cowper, William Francis (*later* Baron Mount-Temple), 77
Cozens, Alexander, 28
Crace & Son, Messrs (decorating firm), 92
Crace, John Dibblee, 92
Crawford, David Alexander Edward Lindsay, 27th Earl of, 117
Crawford, David Alexander Robert, (*earlier* Lord Balniel), 28th Earl of, 128, 131, 141
Crivelli, Carlo: Demidoff Altarpiece, 82; *The Vision of the Blessed Gabriele*, 79
Croker, John, 24
Crowe, Joseph, 72
Curzon (of Kedleston), George Nathaniel Curzon, Marquess: Committee, 103, 108, 110
Cust, Colonel Sir Edward, 46
Cuyp, Aelbert, 84; *The Large Dort*, 87; *The Small Dort*, 87

Dalton, Hugh, Baron, 149
Daniel, Sir Augustus: appointed Director (1928), 119; qualities, 119; relations with Trustees, 121; retires, 122

Darnley, John Stuart Bligh, 6th Earl of, 98
Davies, Sir Martin: joins NG staff, 121; differences with Pope-Hennessy, 126; locks Clark out of library, 128; on care of pictures evacuated during war, 129; catalogue of early Italian collection, 129; Directorship, 143–5; display policy, 143–4
Davies sisters, 116
Degas, Edgar: art sale (1918), 114, 167; *Miss La La at the Cirque Fernando*, 116; *Young Spartans Exercising*, 116
Delacroix, Eugène: *Louis-Auguste Schwiter*, 115; *Ovid among the Scythians*, 140
Delessert, Baron, 84
Dennistoun, James, 66
Desenfans, Noel, 15–17
Devonshire, Evelyn Emily Mary, Duchess of, 22
Dickinson, Goldsworthy Lowes, 119
Disraeli, Benjamin: *Vivien Grey* (novel), 50
Dixon, (Sir) Jeremy, 155–6
Dou, Gerrit: *Portrait of a Man*, 56
Dover, George Agar Ellis, 1st Baron, 20–2, 25, 27–8, 41–3
Dowson, (Sir) Philip, 151
Drouais, François-Hubert: *Madame de Pompadour*, 149
Duccio di Buoninsegna: *The Annunciation* (from *Maestà*), 90; *Jesus opens the Eyes of a Man born Blind* (from *Maestà*), 90; *Maestà*, 117; *Virgin and Child with Saints*, 74, 76
Dulwich College, 17
Dulwich Picture Gallery: opened (1813), 13, 17; design, 156
du Maurier, George: *Trilby* (novel), 95
Duncannon, John William Ponsonby, 1st Baron, 43, 47–8
Dürer, Albrecht: *Saint Jerome*, 162
Düsseldorf: public gallery opened (1710), 13
Dutch Art: 1976 exhibition, 147
Dutch paintings, 84–5, 87
Duveen, Joseph, Baron, 117, 120, 127
Dyce, William: *The National Gallery: its Formation and Management* (report), 65
Dysart House, Pall Mall, 41

Eastlake, Sir Charles Lock: appointed Keeper (1843), 55–6; background and career, 55–6; acquisitions, 56–7, 69–71, 73–6, 79, 170; picture cleaning policy, 58–60; resignation, 60; criticises interiors of NG, 63; appointed Director (1855), 66–8; continental travels, 69, 80; and improved layout to NG, 77; achievements, 78; death, 78, 81; undertakes manuscript catalogue of collection, 79; financial management, 80; identifies Moroni painting, 93; constitutional authority, 166;

Eastlake, Sir Charles Lock (*cont.*): *Materials for a History of Oil Painting*, 60, 76; *Observations on the unfitness of the present building for its purpose*, 57–8
Eastlake, Elizabeth, Lady, 69–71, 80
'Echoes' (PR agency), 127
Edinburgh *see* National Gallery of Scotland
Edward VII, King, 103
Elcho, Francis Charteris, Lord *see* Wemyss, 8th Earl of
Elgin Marbles, 27–8
Ellis, Henry, 37
Ellis, Wynne: bequest to NG, 87–8
'Exhibition of Cleaned Pictures' (1947), 137
Export Reviewing Committee, 144
Eyck, Jan van: *Arnolfini Portrait*, 52–3

Farington, Joseph, 15, 18
Farnborough, Sir Charles Long, 1st Baron, 15–16, 18, 20, 22, 28, 32, 37, 43
Ferrand, Max, 121
Ferrari, Gaudenzio: *Christ Rising from the Tomb*, 97
Fisher, John, Archdeacon of Salisbury, 23
Fitzwilliam Museum, Cambridge, 13, 113, 158
Fitzwilliam, Richard, 7th Viscount, 22
Foggo, George: *The National Gallery: its Pictures and their Painters, with Critical Remarks*, 54
Ford, Richard, 89
Forster, Edward Morgan, 109
Fourment, Helena: Rubens portraits of, 90
Frederick II (the Great), King of Prussia, 13
Frick, Henry Clay, 98, 105
Friedrich, Caspar David: *Winter Landscape*, 154
Friends of the National Gallery, 99
Fry, Margery, 119
Fry, Roger, 101, 114, 116, 119, 125
Fuseli, Henry, 37

Gaddi, Taddeo, 62
Gaertner, Eduard: *The Friedrichsgracht, Berlin*, 154
Gainsborough, Thomas, 139; *Blue Boy*, 115; *The Market Cart*, 38; *Morning Walk*, 140; *Mr. and Mrs. Andrews*, 141; *The Watering Place*, 37
Galvagna, Baron Francesco, 71
Gardner, Isabella Stewart, 98
Garofalo (Benvenuto Tisi da Garofalo): *St Augustine with the Holy Family*, 35
George III, King, 12, 14
Getty, John Paul, 144, 150
Getty Museum, California, 169
Getty, Paul: gift to NG, 150, 160–1
Ghent Altarpiece, 39
Gilpin, William, 35
Giorgione (Giorgio da Castelfranco): misattributions, 128

Giotto (di Bondone): Arena Chapel, Padua, 82
Gladstone, William Ewart, 66, 75, 80
Glasgow, Edwin, 124
Goderich, Frederick John Robinson, Viscount (*later* 1st Earl of Ripon), 23, 32, 42–3
Goethe, Johann Wolfgang von: *Theory of Colours*, 56
Gogh, Vincent: *Chair*, 116; *Sunflowers*, 116; *Wheatfield*, 116
Gombrich, (Sir) Ernst, 142
Gossaert, Jan: *Adoration of the Kings* ('the Castle Howard Mabuse'), 107
Gothic Revival, 52, 123
Gough, Piers, 156
Gould, Cecil, 126, 137
Goya, Francisco de: *Duke of Wellington*, 141
Grand Tour: influence on taste and acquisitions, 19, 33, 36, 53
Grant, Duncan, 114
Great Reform Bill (1832), 45
Gregory, Sir William, 83
Grey, Charles, 2nd Earl, 42
Guercino (Gianfrancesco Barbieri): *Dead Christ Mourned by Two Angels*, 37
Guinness, Sir Edward, 93
Gulbenkian, Calouste: art collection, 137
Gwydir, Peter Robert Burrell, 2nd Baron: sale (1829), 37

Hale, John, 146, 148, 166
Hamilton, William Alexander Douglas-Hamilton, 12th Duke of: art sale (1882), 89
Hamlet, Thomas, 36
Hampton Site, Trafalgar Square, 150–2, 155; *see also* Sainsbury Wing
Hapsburg dynasty, 12
Harcourt, Lewis, 1st Viscount ('Loulou'), 104
Harcourt, Sir William, 97
Harewood, George Henry Lascelles, 7th Earl of, 144
Harman, Jeremiah, 56
Harrison, Frederic, 91
Hawksmoor, Nicholas, 40
Haydon, Benjamin Robert, 27, 31
Hazlitt, William, 19
Henderson, Sir Nicholas, 153
Hendy, Sir Philip: hanging practices, 125, 133–5, 170; appointed Director, 133; and relations with Tate Gallery, 136–7; conservation policy, 137–8, 142; acquisitions, 138, 140–1; differences with Rothenstein at Tate, 139; good relations with Trustees, 166
Heritage Lottery Fund, 161–2
Hermitage Museum *see* St Petersburg

Herringham, Christiana, 99
Heseltine, Michael (*later* Baron), 151
Hobbema, Meindert, 87; *The Avenue*, 84;
  *The Ruins of Brederode Castle*, 84
Hobhouse, John Cam, 24
Hogarth, William, 38, 139; *The Graham
  Children*, 127; *Marriage A-la-Mode*, 18,
  33; *Self Portrait with a Pug*, 18, 37
Holbein, Hans: doubtful attribution, 57; *The
  Ambassadors*, 93; *Christina of Denmark*,
  98, 105; *A Lady with a Squirrel and a
  Starling*, 161
Holford Collection, 117
Holmes, Sir Charles: writes history of NG,
  8; on Burton, 94; on Curzon Committee
  report, 108; on Holroyd's difficulties
  with Trustees, 111; appointed Director
  (1916), 113; acquisitions, 114–17, 167–8;
  background and career, 114; relations with
  Trustees, 117–18, 166; retires (1928), 119;
  and educational role of NG, 171; *Self and
  Others* (autobiography), 117
Holroyd, Sir Charles: appointed Director
  (1906), 101–2; acquisitions, 103–4,
  106, 166; and safeguarding of pictures
  in First World War, 109; Trustees' poor
  relations with, 110–11, 166; resignation
  and death, 112; *Memorandum Regarding
  the Registration of Pictures*, 107; *Some
  Remarks on his Office*, 112
Holwell Carr, Revd William, 36–7
Hooch, Pieter de, 84; *Woman and Her Maid
  in a Courtyard*, 84
Hope, Thomas: Duchess Street Mansion, 19
Hoppner, John, 16
Houghton (house), Norfolk, 13
Hume, Joseph, 43
Huntington, Henry, 115
Huntington Library, California, 121
Huxtable, Ada Louise, 155

Impressionist paintings, 103, 111, 116, 169
Ingres, Jean-Auguste Dominique: *Madame
  Moitessier*, 127–8; *Monsieur de
  Norvins*, 115
Italian Art exhibition (Burlington House,
  1930), 123
Italy: laws on export of works of art, 80, 82

Jaffé, Michael, 158
James, Henry: *The Outcry* (novel), 106
Jameson, Anna: *Companion to the Most
  celebrated Private Galleries of Art in
  London*, 54
John, Augustus: exhibition of drawings
  (1940), 130
Jones, Thomas: *A Wall in Naples*, 161
Jordaens, Jacob, 99
*Journal of Decorative Art*, 92
*Journal of Museum Management and
  Curatorship*, 160

Jowett, Benjamin, 91
Justus of Ghent, 82

Keats, John: 'Ode to a Nightingale', 150
Kensington: Pennethorne recommends
  moving NG to, 66
Kent, William, 40, 44
Keynes, John Maynard, Baron, 114–16
Kingsley, Charles, 61
Klenze, Leo von, 50, 54
Klimt, Gustav: *Portrait of Hermine Gallia*,
  148
Købke, Christen: *The Northern Drawbridge
  to the Citadel in Copenhagen*, 154
Krüger collection, 66
Kugler, F.T., 56, 60
Kurz, Otto, 142

Lanckoroński Collection, 140
Land Fund, 149
Landor, Walter Savage, 39
Landseer, John: *A descriptive . . . catalogue
  of fifty of the earliest pictures*, 39
Lane, Hugh, 103, 110–11
Lansdowne, Henry Charles Keith Petty-
  Fitzmaurice, 5th Marquess of, 97, 99,
  107
Lapeyrière, M. (French tax inspector), 35
Lawrence, Sir Thomas: portrait of
  Angerstein, 7; recommends purchase
  of Rembrandt, 18; portrait of 2nd Earl
  of Liverpool, 28; as Trustee, 32; and
  acquisition of Old Master drawings, 62;
  portrait of Peel's wife, 84
Layard, Sir Austen Henry, 79, 81–4
Legros, Alphonse, 101
Leighton, Frederic, Baron, 90
Leonardo da Vinci: Clark studies, 123;
  *Virgin and Child with St Anne and St John
  the Baptist* ('the Leonardo Cartoon'), 141;
  *The Virgin of the Rocks*, 88
Levey, Sir Michael: favours Skidmore
  design for Hampton Site development,
  152; improves public information, 144;
  appointed Director, 146; character, 146;
  establishes education department, 147;
  early 20th-century acquisitions, 148–9;
  retires, 153; management style, 154; good
  relations with Hale, 166; and range of
  collection, 168; *Painting in Eighteenth-
  century Venice*, 146
Liddell, Henry, 57
Lippi, Filippino: *Virgin and Child with
  Saints Jerome and Dominic*, 73; Rucellai
  Altarpiece, 81
Lippi, Fra Filippo: *Seven Saints*, 79
*Literary Gazette*, 41, 46
Liverpool, Robert Banks Jenkinson, 2nd
  Earl of, 7, 22, 28, 32
Lloyd George, David, 105
Lombardi, Francesco, 73

# Index

London University: extra-mural department collaborates with NG, 147

Londonderry, Charles William Stewart, 3rd Marquess of, 38

Long, Sir Charles see Farnborough, 1st Baron

Longford Castle, near Salisbury, 93

Longleat (estate), Wiltshire, 92

Louvre, Paris: founded, 13; as public institution (1794), 14; authority of Director, 164

Lutyens, Sir Edwin: exihibition (Hayward Gallery, 1981), 156

McColl, Dugald Sutherland, 95, 99

MacGregor, Neil: suggests Cannadine write history of NG, 8; appointed Director, 153; background and career, 153; acquisitions, 154, 161–2; administration, 155; on NG hanging and display, 158, 161; increases visitor numbers, 162; relations with Trustees, 167; and religious content of art, 171

Mackintosh, Sir James, 24

Macpherson (dealer), 83

Mahon, Sir Denis, 126, 154

Manchester: Art Treasures exhibition (1857), 74

Manchester City Art Gallery, 158

Manet, Édouard: Alfred de Rothschild ridicules, 103, 110–11; Corner of a Café-Concert, 116; Execution of Maximilian (fragments), 115; Portrait d'Eva Gonzalès, 103

Manod Quarry, Blaenau Ffestiniog, 129

Mantegna, Andrea: Introduction of the Cult of Cybele at Rome, 85; Triumphs of Caesar, 63; Virgin and Child between the Magdalen and S. John the Baptist, 70

Margarita of Arezzo: The Virgin and Child Enthroned, 74

Marlborough, George Spencer-Churchill, 8th Duke of, 90

Marlborough House, the Mall, 62, 73

Masaccio (Tommaso di Giovanni): St Jerome and John the Baptist (earlier attrib. to Masolino), 140

Massey, Vincent: committee on Tate-NG relations, 136, 138

Mather, Frank, 121

Matisse, Henri: Carmelina, 133

Maximilian II, King of Bavaria, 86

Melozzo da Forli, 81

Memling, Hans: A Young Man at Prayer, 105

Mentmore (house), Buckinghamshire: sale, 149

Methuen, Paul Ayshford Methuen, 4th Baron, 135

Methuen, Paul Sanford Methuen, 3rd Baron, 98

Michelangelo Buonarroti: Entombment, 83; Madonna and Child with St John and the Angels, 57

Miller, John, 155–6

Milton Gallery, London, 37

Mlinaric, David, 159, 161

Monaco, Lorenzo: Adoring Saints (altarpiece), 62

Mond, Frida, 104

Mond, Ludwig: bequest to NG, 104–5, 116, 137

Monteagle, Thomas Spring-Rice, 1st Baron, 31

Moore, Henry, 133

Moore, John, Archbishop of Canterbury, 16

Moore, Morris ('Verax'), 59

Morelli, Giovanni, 82–3

Morgan, John Pierpont, 98, 101

Morland, George, 31

Morning Chronicle, 105

Morning Post, 103, 106

Moroni, Giovan Battista: Portrait of a Gentleman, 93

Morrison, James, 150

Morritt, Major H.E., 102

Mündler, Otto, 69, 71–2, 74–5

Munich: Alte Pinakothek, 49–50, 54, 63

Mure, Colonel Richard, 65

Murillo, Bartolomé Esteban: The Two Trinities, 53

Murray, Charles Fairfax, 89, 117

Mussolini, Benito, 123

Mytens, Daniel: portrait of 2nd Duke of Hamilton, 90

Napoleon I (Bonaparte), Emperor of the French, 19, 24

Nash, John, 40–1, 43, 48

National Art-Collections Fund see Art Fund

National Gallery, London: sense of history, 7; relationship between Directors and Trustees, 10; founding, 12, 14–15, 19–30; funding, 21, 24, 36, 165; and improvement of public taste, 22–3; Constable's opposition to, 23; opening times, 25–6, 78, 127; location in Angerstein's house, 26–7, 39; purpose and motives for founding, 27–30; managed by 'Committee of Six Gentlemen', 32; character and quality of collection, 33, 39; early acquisitions, 34–9, 52–3; British art represented, 37–8, 74, 140, 167; display and hanging of pictures, 39, 50, 74, 124–5, 133–6, 158–61, 169–70; Trafalgar Square building planned, 40–1; design of building, 43–50; new building opened (842), 53–4; Eastlake criticises unfitness of building, 57–8; cleaning of pictures, 58–60, 126, 137–8, 142; popular appeal, 61–2, 64; outgrows accommodation, 63; rebuilding proposals (1850), 63–4;

recommendations on management changes
(1853), 65; Treasury Minute on (27 March
1855), 67–8; proposed move to South
Kensington, 76; closed for alterations
(1860–1), 77; proposed relocation in
Burlington House, 77–8; northward
extension, 78; visitor numbers, 78, 162–3;
competition for building improvements
(1867), 83–4; Barry extension, 87–8, 155,
167; permanent settlement in Trafalgar
Square, 88; buys from British private
collections, 89; main staircase opened, 91;
staircase hall decorated, 92; seeks support
from private individuals, 93; class of
visitors, 94; suffers from foreign galleries'
and collectors' competition, 98, 105–7;
Mond bequest, 104; Salting bequest, 105;
pictures removed to storage in First World
War, 109; Holroyd criticises purchasing
machinery, 112; and acquisition of modern
French art, 115–16; Paramount List,
119; professionalisation of staff, 120–1;
Clark rehangs collection, 124–5; appoints
professional conservator and scientific
laboratory, 126; electric light installed
in galleries, 127; New Exhibition Room,
127; publicity, 127; collection evacuated
in Second World War, 128–9; wartime
concerts and exhibitions, 129–31, 171;
Picture of the Month, 130–1, 171;
damaged in Second World War, 133; air
conditioning installed, 135; picture glass
removed, 135; relations with Tate Gallery,
136, 138–9, 147–9, 168; and conservation
under Hendy, 137–8, 142; modern French
paintings, 140, 169; north galleries opened
(1975), 146–7; education department
established, 147; guide rewritten by
Potterton (1975), 147; acquires early 20th-
century art, 148–9; funding support, 149–
50; purchase grants reduced: (1889), 92;
(1985), 150; development of Hampton Site,
151–2; administrative structure changed
under MacGregor, 154–5; attacked in
*Private Eye*, 159; relationship to state and
government, 164–5; nature and scope of
collection, 167–9; and affordability of art
works, 169; educational role, 170–1; *see
also* Sainsbury Wing; Trustees
National Gallery of Scotland, Edinburgh,
158–9; Sutherland collection on loan to, 15
National Gallery Site Commission, 76
National Heritage Memorial Fund, 149
National Portrait Gallery: acquires land
next to NG, 92; Holmes at, 113–14; and
Hampton Site, 151; facilities improved, 162
National Trust: and Mentmore sale, 149
Nazarenes (group), 55, 86
New York: Metropolitan Museum, 144
Nicholson, Sir William: exhibition (1942),
130

Nicolson, Benedict, 126
Nieuwenhuys, Lambert, 35
*Nineteenth-Century French Painting*
exhibition (1942), 130
Norfolk, Henry Fitzalan-Howard, 15th
Duke of, 105–6
Normanby, Constantine Henry Phipps, 1st
Marquess of, 73
Northcote, James, 16
Northumberland, Alan Ian Percy, 8th Duke
of, 119
Northumberland, Algernon Percy, 10th Earl
of, 119

O'Brien, Sir Patrick, 76
*Observer* (newspaper), 131
Open University: collaboration with NG, 147
Orléans, Louis-Philippe, Duke of: art
collection sold (1798), 14–15, 17–18
Ormsby-Gore, William, 120
Orsi, Lelio: *The Walk to Emmaus*, 97
Ottley, William Young, 38, 39; compiles first
catalogue (1826), 39

Palmerston, Henry John Temple, 3rd
Viscount, 72, 76–7
Panné, Philippe, 33
Panofsky, Erwin, 143
Parmigianino (Girolamo Francesco Maria
Mazzola): *Vision of St Jerome*, 53
Passavant, Johann David, 55; *A Tour of a
German Artist in England*, 69
Pater, Walter, 93
Peel, Sir Robert, 38, 43, 45, 55–9; paintings
collection acquired for NG, 84, 87–8
Pei, I.M. (Partnership), 155
Pembroke, Thomas Herbert, 8th Earl of, 119
Pennethorne, James, 40, 58, 63, 65, 76–8, 92
Penny, Nicholas: *Sixteenth-Century Italian
Paintings*, 8
Penrhyn Castle, Wales, 128–9
Picasso, Pablo: Clark acquires works by, 127;
*Fruit, Bottle and Violin*, 148
Piero della Francesca, 81; *The Baptism of
Christ*, 79; *The Nativity*, 86
Pintoricchio (Bernardino di Betto Vagio):
*Scenes from the Odyssey*, 86
Piper, John: judges competition of
drawings, 147
Pisanello, Antonio: *The Vision of St
Eustace*, 98
Pisani, Conte Vittore, 72
Pitt, William, the Younger, 15–16
Pollaiuolo, Antonio: *Apollo and Daphne*,
87; *Martyrdom of St Sebastian*, 73
Poniatowski, Prince Michael, 15
Pontormo, Jacopo da: *Joseph in Egypt*, 89
Pope-Hennessy, (Sir) John, 126
Potterton, Homan, 147
Pouncey, Philip, 126, 128
Poussin, Gaspard, 53

Poussin, Nicolas, 35, 53; *The Adoration of the Golden Calf*, 138; *A Bacchanalian Revel before a Term*, 36; *Landscape with a Man killed by a Snake*, 138; *The Triumph of Pan*, 150
Poynter, Ambrose, 95
Poynter, Sir Edward: appointed Director, 95; background and career, 95–6; taste and selection, 97, 99, 166; resigns, 100
Prado, Madrid: founded, 13; authority of Director, 164
Pre-Raphaelites, 53
Previtali, Andrea, 128
*Private Eye* (magazine), 159
Property Services Agency, 155
Pucci, Marchese Roberto, 73
Pückler-Muskau, Prince Hermann, 37
Pugin, Augustus Welby Northmore, 49
Purcell Miller Tritton (architects), 161

*Quarterly Review*, 25

Radnor, Jacob Pleydell-Bouverie, 2nd Earl of, 93
Radnor, Jacob Pleydell-Bouverie, 8th Earl of, 144
Radnor, William Pleydell-Bouverie, 5th Earl of, 93
Radnor, William Pleydell-Bouverie, 7th Earl of, 138
Raphael Sanzio: Cartoons, 84; *Ansidei Madonna*, 90–1; *Garvagh Madonna*, 79; *Madonna of the Pinks*, 169; *Mond Crucifixion*, 105; *Portrait of Pope Julius II*, 34; *Saint Catherine*, 52
Rawlins, Ian, 126
Redesdale, Algernon Bertram Freeman-Mitford, 1st Baron, 103, 110
Redon, Odilon: *Ophelia among Flowers*, 148
Rembrandt van Rijn: *The Adoration of the Shepherds*, 34; *A Bearded Man in a Cap*, 56; *The Lamentation over the Dead Christ*, 34; *Margaretha Trip*, 131; *The Mill*, 107; *Renier Anslo*, 98; *A Woman Bathing in a Stream*, 37; *The Woman taken in Adultery*, 18, 34
Reni, Guido: *Jesus and St John*, 56; *Lot and his Daughters leaving Sodom*, 57
Renoir, Pierre Auguste: Clark acquires, 127; *At the Theatre (La Première Sortie)*, 116; *Moulin Huet Bay, Guernsey*, 140; *A Nymph by a Stream*, 140; *Les parapluies*, 103
Reynolds, Sir Joshua, 18, 23, 34, 87, 139; *Colonel Tarleton*, 140; *The Holy Family*, 38; *Mrs Siddons as the Tragic Muse*, 115; *Self-portrait*, 62
Richardson, Mary, 109
Richmond, Charles Gordon-Lennox, 3rd Duke of, 16
Richter, Jean Paul, 104

Ricketts, Charles de Sousy, 113–14
*Rival of Nature, The - Renaissance Painting in its Context* (exhibition, 1975), 148, 162
Robbins, Lionel, Baron, 166
Robinson, Frederick ('Prosperity') *see* Goderich, Viscount
Robinson, John Charles, 79, 81, 98
Rockingham, Charles Watson-Wentworth, 2nd Marquess of, 162
Rogers, Richard, 151
Rogers, Samuel, 38, 43, 71
Rome: public galleries, 20
Roscoe, William, 35
Rosebery, Archibald Philip Primrose, 5th Earl of: Minute transferring acquisition authority to Trustees (1894), 96–7, 166
Ross, Robert, 106
Rossetti, Dante Gabriel, 86
Rothenstein, Sir John, 139
Rothschild, Alfred de, 97, 101–3, 110, 171
Rothschild, Jacob, 4th Baron, 153, 155, 159–60
Rothschild, Nathan Meyer, 1st Baron, 93
Rothschild, Victor, 140–1
Rousseau, Henri (le Douanier): *The Tropical Storm with a Tiger*, 145
Roverselli (Milan dealer), 70
Royal Academy of Arts: founded, 12; and founding of National Gallery, 16; early financing, 24; shares building with NG, 40–1, 44, 46, 49, 77, 167; leaves NG building, 63; relocates to Burlington House, 88; sells Leonardo Cartoon, 141
Royal Academy of Literature, 40
Royal Fine Arts Commission: Eastlake as Secretary, 60
Royal Opera House, Covent Garden, 156
Rubens, Peter Paul: *An Autumn Landscape with a View of Het Steen in the Early Morning*, 34; *Chapeau de Paille*, 84; *The Judgment of Paris*, 57; *Massacre of the Innocents*, 169; *Peace and War*, 59–60; *Portrait of Thomas Howard, Earl of Arundel*, 98, 108; *The Rape of the Sabine Women*, 34; *Samson and Delilah*, 150; *The Watering Place*, 127
Ruhemann, Helmut, 126, 129, 142
Ruisdael, Jacob van: *Extensive Landscape with a Ruined Castle and a Village Church*, 87
Rumohr, Baron von, 55
Ruskin, John: on moral and public improvement, 29, 61; on display of art works, 54, 74; protests at Eastlake's purchase of Reni, 57; on damage to Rubens' *Peace and War* by cleaning, 60; praises Veronese's *Family of Darius*, 72; influence, 93
Russell, Lord John (*later* 1st Earl), 63

Sainsbury Wing: design, 155–7; and hanging of pictures, 170

St Martin-in-the-Fields (church), 45, 47

St Petersburg: Hermitage museum, 49–50

Salisbury, Robert Arthur Gascoyne-Cecil, 3rd Marquess of, 92

Salting, George: bequest to NG, 105

Sanssouci, Potsdam, 13

Sassetta (Stefano di Giovanni): *Scenes from the Life of St Francis*, 127

Sassoon, Sir Philip, 115, 165

Scarpa collection (Milan), 97

Schinkel, Karl Friedrich, 50–1

Scott Brown, Denise (Mrs Robert Venturi), 156–7

Scottish National Gallery *see* National Gallery of Scotland

Sebastiano del Piombo: *The Raising of Lazarus*, 18, 34, 39, 53; *Portrait of a Lady*, 90

Seguier, John, 56, 58

Seguier, William: values Angerstein's collection, 22; appointed first Keeper (1824), 25, 31; duties, 31–2; relations with Trustees, 31; and early acquisitions, 38–9, 52; death, 55

Select Committees, 49, 51–2, 53, 63–5

Seurat, Georges: *Bathers at Asnières*, 116; *The Channel at Gravelines, Grand Fort-Philippe*, 161–2

Shakespeare Gallery, Pall Mall, 16

Shannon, Charles Haslewood, 114

Sheepshanks Collection, 63

Sheridan, Richard Brinsley, 17

Sickert, Walter: exhibition of works (1941), 130

Signorelli, Luca: *Circumcision*, 89; *Triumph of Chastity*, 86

Skidmore, Owings and Merrill (architects), 152

Smirke, Robert, 20–1, 40

Smith, Alistair, 147, 154

Smith, Benjamin, 61

Soane, Sir John, 17, 156

Society of Artists, 12

Society of Dilettanti, 19

Solly, Edward, 51–2

Somaglia family (Milan), 70

South Kensington: proposed as location for NG, 76

South London Art Gallery, Camberwell, 94

Spanish art, 89

Spanton, W.S., 69

Spielmann, Sir Isidore, 106

Stamp, Gavin, 159

Stevens, Alfred, 59

Stirling, James, 156

Stout, George, 137

Strabolgi, David Montague de Burgh Kenworthy, 11th Baron, 135

Stuart-Wortley, John (*later* 2nd Baron Wharncliffe), 21

Stubbs, George, 38; *Whistlejacket*, 162

Studd, Arthur, 139

Sturgis, Alexander, 8–9

Sutherland, George Granville Leveson-Gower, 1st Duke of (*earlier* Earl Gower; *then* Marquess of Stafford)), 15, 19

Sweden: Royal Palace opened to public, 13

Tate Gallery, London: established, 93; Legros appointed first Keeper, 101; report on management, 108; relations with NG, 136, 138–9, 147–8, 168; independence, 138, 140

Tate, Sir Henry, 92–3

Tate Modern, London: opened, 162; government interest in, 165

Tatham, Charles Heathcote, 19

Taylor, Sir John, 91–2

ter Borch, Gerard: *Young Woman playing a Theorbo to Two Men*, 84

Ter Brugghen, Hendrik: *The Concert*, 150

Thackeray, William Makepeace, 50

Thatcher, Margaret, Baroness, 166

Thwaites, Colonel George Saunders, 53

Tiepolo, Giambattista: *An Allegory with Venus and Time*, 144

*Times, The*, 32, 36, 47, 54, 59–60, 89, 101–2, 109, 130

Tintoretto: *Christ washing his Disciple's Feet*, 90; *St George and the Dragon*, 37

Titian: *Bacchus and Ariadne*, 36, 53, 59, 142; *Death of Actaeon*, 144; *Madonna and Child with SS. John the Baptist and Catherine of Alexandria*, 75; *Noli Me Tangere*, 71, 131, 142; *The Rape of Europa*, 98; *Vendramin Family*, 119

Toffoli, Angelo, 71

Trafalgar, Battle of (1805), 16

Trafalgar Square (*earlier* Royal Mews): Nash's plans for, 40–1

*Transfiguration, The* (Russian icon), 116

Travellers' Club, London, 29, 47

*Treasure Houses of Britain, The* (exhibition, National Gallery of Art, Washington), 159

Treasury: allows tax exemption for art works sold to a national collection, 115; fails to spend Land Fund, 149

Trustees: relations with Director, 10, 165–7, 171; first, 32; amateur status, 51–2; role limited by Treasury Minute of 1855, 68; regain authority for acquisition (1894), 96; and 'Lansdowne Resolutions' (on purchasing), 99–100; criticism of Holroyd, 110; relations with Holmes, 117–18; relations with Daniel, 121; relations with Levey, 146; authority and independence, 164–5; monthly meetings, 167

Turner, Joseph Mallord William: style, 23; admires Claude Lorrain, 33;

Turner, Joseph Mallord William (*cont.*):
Bequest, 72–3; reputation, 139; *Dido
building Carthage*, 72; *The Dogana, S
Giorgio, Citella, from the Steps of the
Dogana*, 62; *Sun rising through Vapour*,
72

Uccello, Paolo: *Battle of San Romano*, 74;
*Saint George and the Dragon*, 140
United States of America: art collecting, 88
Uwins, Thomas: appointed Keeper (1847),
61; on visitors' behaviour, 64; on internal
colour scheme, 66; retires, 66

Van Dyck, Sir Anthony: sells Titian's
*Vendramin Family*, 119; *Equestrian
Portrait of Charles I*, 90–1, 124; *Portrait
of George Gage with Two Attendants*, 34;
*Triumph of Silenus*, 84
Velázquez, Diego Rodriguez de Silva y:
*Juan de Pareja*, 144; *Philip IV of Spain
in Brown and Silver*, 89, 126; *Prince
Balthasar Carlos, aged two, with his
Dwarf*, 98; *Rokeby Venus*, 102, 109, 131
Velde, Willem van der, the Younger, 84
Venturi, Robert, 156–7
Vermeer, Jan: *A Young Woman Seated at a
Virginal*, 105
Vernon Collection, 73
Veronese, Paolo: *Adoration of the Kings*, 70;
*The Family of Darius before Alexander*,
71–2
Versailles: Galeries de Batailles, 63
Victoria, Queen: inspects NG building
design, 49; favours J.C. Robinson as
Director, 81

Waagen, Gustav, 51–2, 74
Wales: NG's collection evacuated to in
Second World War, 128–9
Walpole, Sir Robert: art collection, 13
War Artist's Advisory Committee, 130
Warburg Institute: transferred from
Hamburg, 120–1
Warsaw: National Gallery, 15
Warwick, Francis Richard Charles Greville,
5th Earl of, 98
Washington, DC: National Gallery of Art,
159
Waterhouse, Ellis, 121
Weaver, J.R.: chairs Cleaning and Care
committee, 137
Webb, John: bequest, 116
Weenix, Jan Baptist: *A Seaport in Spain*, 90
Wellington, Arthur Wellesley, 1st Duke of,
22, 41, 48

Wemyss, Francis Charteris, 8th Earl of
(*earlier* Lord Elcho), 72, 91
Wernher Collection, 150
West, Benjamin, 14
Westminster, Hugh Lupus Grosvenor, 1st
Duke of, 91
Westminster, Hugh Richard Arthur
Grosvenor, 2nd Duke of, 115
Weyden, Rogier van der: *The Magdalen
Reading*, 75
Wheeler, Charles, 130
Whistler, James McNeill: Boxall admires,
81; exhibition of works (1941), 130;
*Nocturne: Black and Gold - The Fire
Wheel*, 139; *Nocturne: Blue and Silver
- Cremorne Lights*, 139; *Symphony in
White, No.2: The Little White Girl*, 139
Whitechapel Art Gallery, 94, 155
Whitehead, Chris: *The Public Art Museum
in Nineteenth Century Britain*, 8
Widener, Joseph, 107
Wilhelm, Prince of Orange, 21
Wilkes, John, 12
Wilkie, David, 31; *The Village Holiday*, 37
Wilkins, William, 41; design of NG, 43–91,
53, 58, 76, 151, 159; *A Letter to Lord
Viscount Goderich* (1831), 42
William IV, King, 50
Williams-Wynne, Watkin, 138
Wilson, Michael, 154
Wilson, Richard: Hendy acquires paintings
by, 140; *The Destruction of the Children
of Niobe*, 37; *A Distant View of
Maecenas' Villa*, 37
*Wilton Diptych*, 119
Witt, Sir Robert, 99
Wittkower, Rudolph, 127
Woodburn, Samuel, 62
Wordsworth, William, 20, 39
World War II (1939–45), 128–30
Wornum, Ralph, 68–9, 75, 77–8, 83;
*Outline of a General History of Painting
amongst the Ancients*, 69
Wouwermans, Philips, 84
Wright, Joseph (of Derby), 38
Wyatt, James, 40

Yamanaka & Co. (art dealers), 117
Yeats, Jack: exhibition (1942), 130

Zurbaran, Francisco de: *Cup of Water and a
Rose on a Silver Plate*, 162
Zwinger Gallery, Dresden, 12